KOS

CW01507616

Travel with Marco Polo Insider Tips

INSIDER TIP
Your shortcut to a great experience

MARCO POLO
TOP HIGHLIGHTS

CASTLE OF THE KNIGHTS OF ST JOHN NERÁTZA ⭐
Views from medieval battlements over the city and harbour to distant hills make this fort unique.

➤ p. 42, Kos Town

CASA ROMANA ⭐
This ancient villa, once owned by a wealthy Roman, is every bit as majestic as a Hollywood star's mansion.

➤ p. 47, Kos Town

WESTERN EXCAVATION ZONE ⭐
Mosaics take you back to the colourful world of antiquity, including an ancient beauty contest.
📷 Tip: The mosaic colours are particularly vivid after it has rained.

➤ p. 48, Kos Town

MARKET HALL ⭐
Here you will find the country's delicacies for your next picnic or for a taste of Kos at home.
📷 Tip: Take close-ups of individual items and turn them into a collage later on.

➤ p. 54, Kos Town

EMBRÓS THÉRME ⭐
Wellness for free: relax in the natural stone basin below high cliffs where thermal and sea waters mix.

➤ p. 57, Kos Town

PLATÍA OF PLATÁNI ⭐
Which is better, Turkish or Greek cuisine? Judge for yourself on this village square.
📷 Tip: The square is especially beautiful at night when the lights come on.

➤ p. 58, Kos Town

ASKLÍPION ⭐7

Once upon a time, the gods gave advice here on health and well-being. Today, you will have to rely on your own inner voice.
📷 *Tip: Crouch in front of the column stump with an altar slab on the upper terrace and use the Turkish coastline as a backdrop.*

➤ p. 60, Kos Town

LAGOÚDI ⭐8

First, visit the church with the priest; then, sit down in the artisan café run by a Flemish woman. You won't find a more peaceful mountain village on the entire island!
📷 *Tip: The friendly priest will always be happy to have a selfie taken with you.*

➤ p. 78, The Centre

OLD PÝLI ⭐9

Enjoy a walk through the forest to the romantic castle ruins with sea views.

➤ p. 80, The Centre

ÁGIOS STÉFANOS BASILICA ⭐10

The one place you can visit a church in your bikini. This old basilica without a roof is situated right on a beautiful beach (see photo).

➤ p. 90, The West

CONTENTS

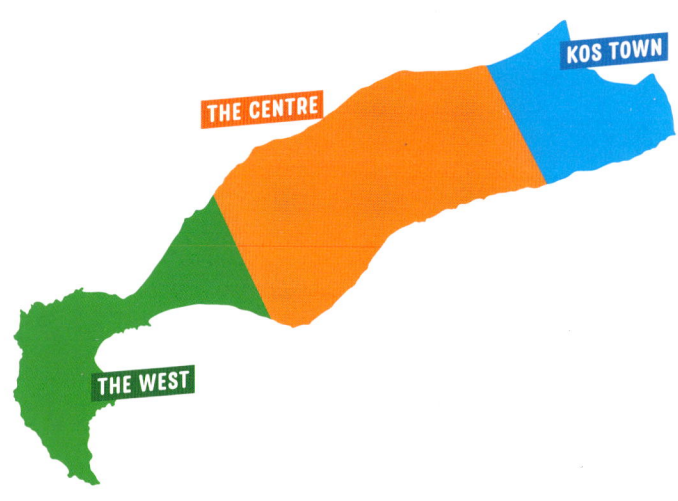

CONTENTS

☉	Plan your visit	🍴	Eating/drinking
€–€€€	Price categories	👜	Shopping
(*)	Premium-rate phone number	🍸	Going out
		🐾	Top beaches

(💷 A2) Refers to the removable pull-out map
(💷 a2) Refers to the additional map on the pull-out map
(0) Located off the map

BEST OF
KOS

A charming taverna terrace in Old Pýli

BEST

WHEN IT RAINS

ACTIVITIES TO BRIGHTEN YOUR DAY

JUST DIVE IN

Make use of a rainy day to visit the *Liámis Dive Centre*, which offers trial dive courses in safe coves as well as adventurous trips to wrecks and sea caves.

➤ p. 33, Kos Town

ESCAPE TO ANTIQUITY

You are guaranteed to stay dry in the *Archaeological Museum* in Kos Town, where you can dicover marble gods and heroes whose wild myths will make your hair stand on end.

➤ p. 45, Kos Town

RAIN OR SHINE …

… the merchants in the shop-lined alleyways of *Odós Iféstou* and *Odós Apelloú* are open for business. Dozens of shops offer their wares to those fleeing the raindrops.

➤ p. 53, Kos Town

ORIENTAL WELL-BEING

At *Artemis Hamam & Spa* in Tigáki, you can experience the rituals of a Turkish bath in a modern setting and smell the aromatic hookah at the *Garden Bar*.

➤ p. 69, The Centre

CLOUD LANDSCAPE

A rain shower on Kos can be an exciting experience. Clouds rush across the island and engulf the landscape, and lightning flashes across the mountains of Anatolia. Some of the best seats for this celestial spectacle can be found at the *Sunset Balcony* in Zía.

➤ p. 77, The Centre

KOS WITHOUT THE TOURISTS

If you want to see how older Koans lived when they were children, visit the *windmill* in Antimáchia and the nearby *Traditional House*. The mill's café serves coffee and cake that is baked with their own milled flour.

➤ p. 81, The Centre

BEST ON A BUDGET

FOR SMALLER WALLETS

CATACOMBS BENEATH THE THEATRE

Not only is a visit to the *Roman theatre* in Kos Town free – in the *Odéon* (see photo) you can even climb down into the catacombs.

➤ p. 47, Kos Town

SPA WITH A DIFFERENCE

At *Embrós Thérme*, thermal water at a temperature of 45°C flows into the sea. In an improvised pool among the rocks you will find people (mostly Greek) taking a free thermal bath.

➤ p. 57, Kos Town

ART AT A HOTEL

Even if you're not staying at the *Neptune Resort*, you can still admire the works of Peter R. Müller for free. On the premises of one of the island's best hotels, the Bavarian artist has created *sculptures* of deities and heroic figures from Greek mythology.

➤ p. 72, The Centre

GOOD WINE FOR ALL

In restaurants, excellent Greek wines tend to be expensive, whereas at vineries and in wine stores, such as *Deligusto* in Kardámena, you can get great wines at reasonable prices.

➤ p. 83, The Centre

MINI OASIS

Situated on the road between the airport and Kéfalos, the *Fytório* taverna – like a mini oasis in the desert – serves food for much less than beach-side establishments. You are welcome to stroke and feed the donkeys next door.

➤ p. 91, The West

WHERE TO SHOP

Holidaymakers in the beach resorts along the northern coast can get groceries from the large *Constantínos* supermarkets, on the access roads to Marmári and Tigáki, for only a little more money than from their global competitors near Kos Town.

BEST

WITH CHILDREN

FUN FOR YOUNG & OLD

TRIPS ON THE CHOOCHOO TRAIN

Trenáki (small train) is what the Greeks call the mini train with two or three open carriages on rubber wheels that ply the roads of many Greek holiday resorts (see photo). Kos boasts three; one starts from Mandráki Harbour in the island's capital for tours of the town, another leaves hourly from the central bus station for a trip to Asklípion, while the third runs in Kardámena on the southern coast.

➤ p. 54, Kos Town

GO KARTS FOR ANY AGE

Chrístos Go Karts at Marmári lets the whole family, whatever their age, put their foot to the throttle. There are separate tracks for toddlers, under-tens, and those aged ten and above.

➤ p. 70, The Centre

ERIKA'S HORSE FARM

Erika's Horse Farm comprises stables, a café, a playground and a petting zoo.

When riding on the beach, the little ones are in the saddle with an adult alongside, and the farm also offers pony rides elsewhere. There are evening carriage rides in Marmári, too.

➤ p. 70, The Centre

GREEN & PLEASANT

Natural Park Zia is a pretty forest park with plenty to entertain the children, including a playground and animal petting. Your ticket even allows you to come and go throughout the day.

➤ p. 77, The Centre

GIANT WATER SLIDES

Your hotel doesn't have a water park? Don't worry: the island has public water parks with both short and long slides, such as *Aquatica* in Kardámena on the south coast.

➤ p. 83, The Centre

BEST
CLASSIC EXPERIENCES

ONLY ON KOS

TRULY PUBLIC

Have you ever been present at a court session? From the *kafeníon* next to the courthouse in Kos Town, you can enjoy a mocha *and* follow court proceedings through the open doors.

➤ p. 51, Kos Town

OTTOMAN CUISINE

The tavernas on the village square in *Platáni* nearly all bear Turkish names because Kos and Rhodes are the only Greek islands where Muslims originally from Turkey still have their home. The spicy Turkish dishes here are an experience for the palate.

➤ p. 58, Kos Town

COWS ON THE BEACH

On Kos, cows can appear omnipresent. You find them in the countryside, on the beach or in the odd quiet alleyway. There are large numbers in the area between Tigáki and Mastichári.

➤ p. 68, p.69, The Centre

SUNSETS

Kos offers dreamy sunsets almost every evening. The most popular locations for watching the sun go down are the many tavernas in the mountain village of *Zía* on the slopes of the island's highest peak. We recommend that you book a table in advance, for example at the *Oromédon*.

➤ p. 77, The Centre

CELEBRATE TOGETHER

The small Koan churches located outside the villages usually have an area reserved for festivities with long tables and benches. If you are visiting Kos in mid-August, you can watch more than 1,000 locals eat, drink and party together after the service on the church feast day on the square at *Panagía Stylóti church* near Kéfalos.

➤ p. 95, The West

GET TO KNOW KOS

Cats on Níssiros, the small volcanic island south of Kos

DISCOVER KOS

If you like cycling, you will love Kos with its wide cycle paths and gentle ascents

The moment your plane starts to descend, you'll see the Greek islands spread out below, and, if you are sitting on the left, you can look far into Turkey. Already, from the air, you will see that Kos has long sandy beaches, lots of greenery, and not a huge hotel in sight. And given the perfect size of the island, you can be relaxing in the sea just two hours after landing!

Tourism is the main source of income. There is no industry to speak of, and farming is mainly restricted to the cultivation of grain, wine and olives and the keeping of cows or sheep. The island recently had to cope with three crises. In 2009, the economic and financial crisis hit the whole of Greece. Then followed the refugee crisis in 2015/16; the unfair representation of the crisis and its impact in the media contributed to a significant drop in tourism, especially on Kos. In the summer of 2017, a severe earthquake left two people dead, and Kos was again the

1150–750 BCE
Kos is settled by the Dorians, a Greek tribe

750–490 BCE
Archaic era, emergence of the Greek city states

490–336 BCE
Classical era. In 460 BCE, physician Hippocrates is born on Kos

336–82 BCE
Hellenistic era

82 BCE–CE 395
Kos forms part of the Roman Empire

CE 395–1307
Kos belongs to the Eastern Roman Byzantine Empire

victim of negative publicity. However, Kos has now become one of Greece's top destinations once again.

AN ISLAND FOR CYCLISTS

All the while, Kos has worked hard to keep its guests happy. Identifying and implementing environmental trends early on, Kos has been promoting bike use for years. As practically all holiday resorts and beach hotels are situated on the flat plain along the northern coast, cycling requires no great effort. Wide cycle paths and roads with little traffic run parallel to the sea, making the bike an ideal mode of transport for all. At times, paths cut across fields of grain that are harvested as early as May and then used as cow pastures or to cultivate melons. Others paths lead along low dunes, tempting passers-by for an impromptu swim. Again and again, you'll discover shady groves of trees right by the sea, perfect for a short rest. Many tavernas along the way have installed bike stands. Only hikers still baffle the Koans. That somebody would walk when they don't have to is still a mystery to them, and therefore signposted and well-maintained hiking trails are the exception rather than the rule on Kos.

LOW-COST TRANSPORT

Another exemplary initiative is the public transport network. Town bus services connect the surrounding beach hotels with the capital until late at night, and overland buses link Kos Town with villages and beaches. This means getting around doesn't have to involve spending much money or polluting the atmosphere. Even take-away copies of bus timetables are available, something

1307-1523
The Knights of St John occupy the Dodecanese

1523
Ottoman rule

1912
Italy conquers the Dodecanese

1947
The Dodecanese becomes part of Greece

1981
Greece becomes a member of the EU

2010-18
The Greek debt crisis

2022
Visitor numbers recover and exceed pre-Covid 19 figures

practically unheard of in other parts of Greece. Within the town area, the bus stops have numbers, meaning you don't have to memorise complicated names.

SIGÁ, SIGÁ – TAKE YOUR TIME

A certain serenity is a fundamental characteristic of most Koans. The mad rush is an alien concept to them. This is visible in the cafés, where statistically they make a single cup of coffee last an average 94 minutes, and in the tavernas, where they

INSIDER TIP
More talking, less walking

lavishly dine the night away. Koans would never consider going on an English-style pub crawl or moving from one tapas bar to the next, like the Spanish do. Too much moving around would hinder their chats with friends – and that to the Greeks is what

going out is about first and foremost.

FANTASTIC NATURE

The natural environment of Kos is not spectacular as such, but it is surprisingly green and varied. At an altitude of 846m, the Mount Díkeos mountain range, while dropping off steeply and inaccessibly towards the southern coast, doesn't stand comparison with the wild mountains that dominate the mainland or Crete.

INSIDER TIP
Ideal hiking country

After rainy winters and far into the spring, hundreds of flamingos visit the saline lake of Tigáki. In the narrow valleys in the centre of the island, flower meadows and wild artichokes can blossom undisturbed. And on the green Kéfalos peninsula, visitors can hike for hours and will only meet a few farmers or shepherds. The

near-treeless landscape allows the gaze to wander far across the land, so that despite the lack of signposting nobody gets lost. The only time it gets lonelier still on Kos is between mid-October and early May, when the vast majority of tourists have left. During that period, businesses that rely on tourism remain closed, and many Koans choose to do some travelling themselves.

BEST MEDICINE

The island's most famous son, Hippocrates, is from Kéfalos in the quiet west of the island. Born in 460 BCE, he is considered the "father of medicine". On Kos, Hippocrates founded a medical school that functioned for nearly 1,000 years. Looking at illnesses no longer as trials sent by the gods, he researched their origins instead. Hippocrates prescribed natural medicines, but also found a clever way to involve the gods in his therapies, interpreting the dreams of his patients as divine counsel, helping to trigger psychosomatic processes of self-healing. Hippocrates's teaching was so successful that, following his death, the Asklípion was erected in his honour, turning Kos into one of the largest centres of healing in the ancient world. This important historical site can be found on the edge of Kos Town. Even those travelling to Kos just for sun and sea should not miss this unique mixture of temple complex and hospital, in a spot with beautiful views to boot.

AT A GLANCE

33,300
inhabitants

Isle of Man: 84,200

70

taxis operate on Kos

120km
of coastline

Isle of Man: 160km

290km²
area

Isle of Man: 572km²

HIGHEST PEAK:
DÍKEOS
843m

Snaefell on the
Isle of Man: 620m

WARMEST MONTH
JULY
33°C

Month with the
most rainfall
JANUARY

Kos: 92mm
Isle of Man:
102mm

VISITORS

In 2022, more than 1.5 million passengers
landed at Kos Airport

COWS

Approx. 300 cows live on Kos, many of
which are kept tethered in the fields. If
you would like to donate money for
proper fencing, visit *gasah.ch*.

VIP BIRTHS
Cleopatra gave birth to her
youngest son on Kos

14KM
SEPARATE KOS FROM
TURKEY

UNDERSTAND KOS

A NOBLE BAKER
In the late summer of 2015, at the height of the refugee crisis, 76-year-old baker Dioníssis Arvanitákis from Kos hit the headlines for giving away 100kg of bread every day to refugees arriving at the island's harbour. The prime minister of Luxembourg praised him for being an exemplary European citizen, and he was also given a European award.

TWO MEN AT A TABLE
Two men sit at a table, huddled over a board with two tiny dice and thick round plastic discs in two different colours. Their heads are bowed together in concentration, muscles taut, and they are often surrounded by a crowd of spectators. The game is *távli*, the Greek version of backgammon, and is a part of the Greek way of life for many of the island's men and some young Greek women. Almost every café and many bars have a spare board for you to play – simply Google the rules of the game.

TWELVE ISLANDS
Nitpickers will object: Kos belongs to the Dodecanese archipelago, whose Greek name *Dodekaníssia* means "12 islands". In reality, the Dodecanese includes 19 inhabited islands, from Kastellórizo in the east to Kassos in the west via Rhodes and Kos to Pátmos and its satellite islands Arkí, Agathoníssi and Maráthi. The regional government works out of Rhodes.

DIVINE INTERVENTION
If you are ever in trouble and need a helping hand, you could try doing as the locals do and make the sign of the cross on your chest (using only the right hand, join your thumb and first two fingers and lay the last two fingers flat against your palm then move your hand up-down-right and left) and whisper your wish to the appointed saint. Christóphoros grants a safe journey by land, Nikólaos protects seafarers, Fanoúrios is called upon to find lost persons and objects, and Markélla to cure hip problems. The Virgin Mary, the *Panagía*, can help in all situations.

HOLIDAYS AT THE CLUB
These days, over 70 per cent of all hotel beds on Kos are in all-inclusive resorts. Some visitors love this kind of holiday, and it has brought the island above-average rates of bed occupancy. However, many Greeks are demanding a ban on this system, which they call *clubs*. As the tourists' money is mostly spent in the resorts, quite a few cafés and tavernas in the tourist centres have had to close or have experienced a steep fall in profits, while all-inclusive resorts create only low levels of local employment.

BYZANTINE ROOTS
You will encounter the word "Byzantine" on thousands of brown signs dotted all over Kos. The

Why not try a game of *távli* in a relaxed café with coffee and cake?

Byzantine Empire was the continuation of the Roman Empire in the East from around 500 to 1453, roughly the same period as our Middle Ages. Until 1307, Kos belonged to this empire, which spread across all of Asia Minor, the Balkans and Greece. Its capital city was Constantinople, which became Istanbul when it fell to the Ottomans in 1453. Many Greeks would like to see a return to this period, which is why the yellow and black Byzantine flag can be seen flying in front of many churches and monasteries on Kos. The island also serves as the residence for the Orthodox patriarch, the equivalent of the Catholic pope.

FAMOUS DOCTOR

In its long history, Kos has only produced one celebrity, namely the physician Hippocrates. He was born in 460 BCE in what is today Kéfalos. Considered one of the most influential figures in the history of medicine, he is often referred to as the "Father of Medicine" in recognition of his contributions to the field as the founder of the Hippocratic School of Medicine. He is also credited with coining the Hippocratic Oath, still taken by physicians all over the world today.

NO HASTE

Do you know what tomorrow will bring? Do as the Koans do and don't waste your time planning for the long term. Unlike in northern Europe, large events and festivals are only made public a few days in advance. When it comes to arranging an appointment, vague plans to meet the following morning, afternoon, evening or even next week are made, adding the all-important *"ta léme"* – "We'll talk again later." You can then expect a call one hour beforehand to confirm the exact time – give or take the customary half an hour.

FOUR-LEGGED FRIENDS IN CRISIS

All over Kos you'll see dogs and cats roaming freely in villages and towns and in many tavernas. The animals are harmless, but they have a hard life and go hungry, particularly in winter.

In addition, the financial crisis has led to an increase in the number of pedigree dogs being abandoned in the wild or on refuse tips. The *Kivótos* charity *(FB: Animal Rescue Kos)* cares for these animals, runs a small rescue centre, is always looking for sponsors and tries to find new homes for these stray animals.

FORERUNNER OF THE EU

Did you know that a European "union" of sorts existed 700 years ago? And its capital was not Brussels but Rhodes? From this base, the Order of the Knights of St John (or Knights Hospitaller) ruled over several islands in the eastern Mediterranean, including Kos, from 1307 to 1521. The Order consisted of knights from all over Christian Europe who lived peacefully

From the movie into the clubs: the *sirtaki* was choreographed for Alexis Zorba

with one another and elected a ruler who served for life. Although nationality was subordinate to membership of the Order, the knights were organised into groups, or "langues", based on their language and place of origin. In 1530 the Knights of St John relocated to the island of Malta.

BUSHY BEARDS & LONG HAIR

The dress code of Greek Orthodox priests has changed little in five centuries: whether out shopping with their wife and children or out walking, the priests are always obliged to wear their long black robes. They are allowed to marry; celibacy is only expected of bishops and those above them. The *pappádes* have three other essential items: a tall black hat, hair worn in braids and a signature bushy beard. God is supposed to stunt hair loss. *Pappádes* are a common sight, even in coffee shops and tavernas. Their profession is "crisis-proof" because they are paid by the state.

RARELY ALONE

Koans do not generally like spending time on their own – even cosy twosomes are reserved for a certain hour of the day. Greeks prefer a *paréa*: a group of friends or acquaintances who regularly meet up to drink coffee or eat, go clubbing and on holiday together. The question asked by friends after an event or gathering is not what was the hotel or food like, but how was the *paréa*?

If you do have to go it alone – whether in the car or in the fields – you will always be accompanied by the

TRUE OR FALSE?

ALL KOANS DANCE THE SIRTAKI

It was Hollywood star Anthony Quinn who made the *sirtaki* famous around the world. Ever since he danced it in the 1964 film *Zorba the Greek*, every non-Greek thinks of it as an ancient Greek dance. In reality, it was choreographed specifically for this movie because real Greek folk dances were considered too complicated for the US audience. However, during the "dance along" stage of "Greek nights" in holiday resorts, it continues to get tourists up on the dancefloor.

ALL KOANS ARE WELL OFF

Although you will see few people begging in Kos Town, you should not conclude that there is no poverty on the island. Junior solicitors get paid a mere 600 euros per month, teachers receive 800 euros and waiters about 900 euros plus tips. Many pensioners are forced to get by on 400 euros per month. Social security is insufficient too, with unemployment benefits only being paid after someone has been working continuously for six months; even then, job seekers only get three payments of 400 euros in winter.

island's saints. They are present in the form of icons wherever you go – either as printed images or painted on church and chapel walls and hanging on walls on the sides of the road. You know you are always in safe hands and in good company.

WEBSITES – YESTERDAY'S NEWS

Although Kos websites are usually creative in design, they often lack up-to-date information and news. Admittedly, it's hard work maintaining a homepage, which is why many of the restaurant and café owners in Kos have switched to Facebook, Instagram, LinkedIn, etc. for posting events and live acts. Hoteliers prefer to pay commission fees of up to 20 per cent to accommodation websites like booking.com and airbnb.com rather than engaging the services of professional web agencies.

CRISIS PROOF

It appears that the Greeks bear their crises with greater ease than many other Europeans, and there may even be some oriental fatalism involved. Over the past 75 years, the Hellenes have suffered hard times significantly more often than other Europeans. First there was the Civil War from 1946 to 1949, during which more Greeks died than in World War II. Then, from 1967 to 1974, a brutal military junta ruled over the country. And more recently, the EU partners and the IMF have exercised heavy pressure on the Greeks because of their near bankruptcy. Following the global economic crisis in 2008, the country was forced to cut pensions, wages and social spending, while

having to increase taxes and sell many state-owned assets to foreign entities. At times, unemployment was above 25 per cent – 50 per cent among young people. When, finally, the country emerged from its economic and financial crisis, it was hit by the Coronavirus pandemic. And when tourism picked up again, Putin's troops invaded Ukraine. Despite all these calamities, the Greek people have not become disheartened, and in 2022 were finally able to report record numbers of tourists.

NEIGHBOURLY RELATIONS

Privately, most Greeks and Turks get on well, and their cuisine, music and dances are similar. Koan pub landlords always look forward to groups of Turkish visitors because of their willingness to spend money in bars and restaurants. However, there have been problems caused by Turkish politicians who sent fighter jets and drones into the Greek airspace, openly threatened Greece with violence at election rallies and claimed numerous Greek islands for Turkey because of suspected natural resources under the seabed.

GIVE & TAKE

Overall, Kos is a pretty clean island, although you find a lot of rubbish in harvested fields and on unmanaged beaches. However, you can do your bit: there is a group of 10,000 people called *Kos We Care* who organise regular litter picks involving locals and holidaymakers alike. Visit Facebook *(Kos We Care)* for current dates. A tip

Icons represent heaven on earth and are venerated as much as the saints themselves

for smokers: bring your own pocket ashtray!

RELIGION

Apart from a small Muslim minority on the islands of Kos and Rhodes, and in Western Thrace on the mainland, as well as small Jewish communities in the big cities, nearly all Greeks profess allegiance to Greek Orthodox Christianity. Orthodox Christians don't recognise the pope in Rome as the head of Christianity, holding this claim to be the work of the devil. Having developed their belief system from early Christendom and not changed it since the ninth century, they feel a strong connection with and allegiance to the Apostles and early Christians. Orthodox Christians categorically refute the God-given character of the dogmas proclaimed by the Roman Catholic pope while also decrying the work of the Protestant reformers.

ENERGY FOOTPRINT

Although there is a will, the way is obstructed by a lack of funding. With no incineration plant and, thankfully, no nuclear power plant on the island, the only power plant is an old site to the west of Mastichári. Alternative forms of energy? There is just one large wind park near Kéfalos. Solar panels on houses and hotels are a more common sight on the island, and reward the average man with the direct benefits of going green.

EATING
SHOPPING
SPORT

Holiday between the pool and the sea in northwest Kos

EATING & DRINKING

In the evenings, Koans hardly ever go out to dinner on their own. For them, the companionship of a happy table, the *paréa*, is more important than any culinary delights; this is why there are so many large tables at the tavernas.

EVERYTHING SHARED BY ALL
It is rare for someone to order a dish just for themselves. The Greeks love their *mezedákia*, placing various small dishes in the centre of the table. They arrive in no fixed order – dishes are served when the kitchen has cooked them. Everyone gets an empty plate, so people can take what and how much they like. This way, you don't need separate children's portions; you just give them what they like best. Meat and fish are usually served on large platters to share too.

Very often, a *paréa* will order a lot more than they can actually eat: to devour everything is seen as embarrassing, as it shows that not enough food has been ordered. All plates, even the empty ones, would usually stay on the table. Waiters don't clear the table so the *paréa* can see at all times how well they have feasted.

INSIDER TIP
Never clear your plate!

ILLUSTRATED MENUS
The Greeks prefer to have the waiter list what the kitchen has to offer on the day and to discuss the finer points. Menus are almost always multilingual, and in tourist hotspots are often illustrated with photographs. Beware: when the dishes arrive, they usually look completely different from the pictures.

TRY OUT NEW THINGS
Famous Greek specialities, such as moussaka and souvlaki appear on

most menus on Kos. More unusual Greek dishes are worth trying too, though. While you don't have to go for grilled lamb's head *(kefalákia),* other great culinary discoveries could include tripe soup *(patsá),* chickpea purée, *(fáva),* or fish egg purée *(taramá).*

Rarer, and also delicious, are *anthoús,* courgette flowers filled with rice and herbs. An excellent Hellenic alternative to the classic Greek salad is *chórta,* a salad from cooked wild plants such as chard, dandelion or coltsfoot leaves.

SNACKS & SWEET DELIGHTS
Nearly all restaurants and tavernas are open all day long. Often, English breakfast is served from 10am onwards; main meals are usually available at any time between 11am and midnight. For a small snack or on days when you want to save some money, a *psistaría* (small snack restaurant) will offer a good alternative.

Visitors with a sweet tooth will want to head for a Greek pastry bakery, *zacharoplastío,* serving mainly eastern specialities alongside cream tarts and sponge cakes. Make sure you try *loukoumádes* if they are on offer: always freshly deep-fried in oil, these doughnuts are sprinkled with honey and cinnamon or icing sugar.

ISLAND WINES
For a long time, tourists were regarded as more lucrative than grapes on Kos. Koans only grew vines for their own consumption, while importing bottled wines from other regions of the country. It was only at the turn of the millennium that young Koans returned to making wine on a large scale. Since then, seven small wineries have been producing more than 30 different bottled wines. Two large

Vineyard near Kos Town

mixed with water. The best Greek ouzo brands are said to be distilled at Plomári on the island of Lesbos further north; for example, *Plomarioú*, *Mini* and *Barbayiannis*. Another after-dinner pick-me-up is *Metaxá* brandy, available in various qualities.

Fashionable once again is *mastícha*, from the island of Chíos – a liqueur that gets its aroma from the resin of the mastic shrub. It provides the basic ingredient for many modern Greek cocktails. A renaissance is also being experienced by the almost-black *tentoúra*, from the Peloponnese. It's a type of bitter with an aroma of cloves, cinnamon and nutmeg.

ORDERING COFFEE

The Greeks drink coffee all day long, on any occasion. However, ordering coffee in Greece is a bit of an art form. To start with there is the choice between Greek mocha, known as *kafé ellinikó*; hot instant coffee, usually called *ness sestó*; and cold *frappé* or instant coffee beaten to a froth and served with ice cubes.

Also, don't forget to state the degree of sweetness you'd like, as the water is boiled together with the coffee and sugar: *skétto*, no sugar; *métrio*, with a little sugar; *glikó*, with a lot of sugar. Greek coffee is always drunk without milk. If you'd like your hot or cold Nescafé with milk, add the words *me gála*. The same applies to fashionable iced coffee drinks such as *freddo espresso* or *freddo cappuccino*, appreciated mainly by young consumers.

businesses near Tigáki predominantly use international grapes, such as Merlot, Syrah, Chardonnay and Grenache. *Triandafyllópoulos (kos winery.gr)*, who are also experimenting with old autochthonous grapes, are the market leader, followed by *Hatziemmanouil (hatziemmanouil.gr)*. Recently, the family-run *Mesariano* winery at the western edge of Kos Town has started to offer organic wine. Organic wine is also sold by the *Pétra Marinoú* winery, which is located between Linopóti and Pýli. *Skevosilax* winery near Lagada Beach in the west of the island produces the only wines in the Kéfalos region.

OUZO & CO.

In terms of alcohol, the Greek national drink is ouzo, an aniseed liqueur which is taken either neat, on ice or

Today's specials

Starters

FÁVA
Purée made from yellow split peas with onions and olive oil

NOUBOÚLO
Mildly smoked ham

TARAMÁ
Reddish or white purée made from fish roe

Salads

CHORIÁTIKI
Mixed salad with olives and feta cheese

CHÓRTA
Salad made from cooked leaves of wild plants or chard

PATSÁRIA
Beetroot, served cold as a salad or lukewarm and including the vitamin-rich leaves as a vegetable

Meat

BEKRÍ MEZÉ
Mildly spicy pork goulash braised in red wine

JUVÉTSI
Oven-baked pasta (that looks a bit like rice) with beef

PASTISÁDA
Braised beef with pasta and tomato sauce

SOFRÍTO
Beef marinated in vinegar and braised in red wine

Fish

BAKALJÁROS ME SKORDALJÁ
Dried hake *(merluza)*, served with a potato-garlic purée

BOURDÉTTO
A peppery fish soup, either with *skórpios* (scorpionfish) or *pastanáka* (stingray)

GALÉO ME SKORDALJÁ
Boneless houndshark with a potato and garlic purée

MARÍDES
Crispy fried anchovies, eaten whole (with head and tail)

SHOPPING

When it comes to souvenirs, expect the biggest dent in your wallet to come from the many jewellery shops in the island's towns. Even the smaller seaside resorts and hotels have a selection of them. Otherwise, your money is not in danger of running out, as Koans make almost nothing themselves, apart from food and drink. Virtually everything is imported – in the best case from other regions in Greece, but sometimes from the Far East.

SIMPLY DELICIOUS

Fruit marinated in syrup, which you can get in the market hall in Kos Town, is a truly Koan delicacy. There you will also find many specialities from other Greek regions. Thyme honey and dried herbs could well be from Kos, while the saffron on offer derives mostly from the northern Greek town of Kozáni. If you take a trip to the neighbouring island of Níssiros, make sure to get a small bottle each of *kaneláda* cinnamon lemonade and *soumáda* almond milk, as well as the natural pumice.

FASHION & SHOES

For fashionable clothes, most Koans go to Rhodes or straight to Athens. Kos doesn't offer a wide selection. This doesn't mean you can't make some good fashion discoveries. Take a stroll through the shops along Odós Venizélou and Odós Xanthoú in Kos Town, keeping an eye out for the shoe shops that stock extravagant Greek designs. A wide selection of vegan shoes is available from *Mouzákis* on Platía Konítsis, where Greek-Austrian owners Giórgos and Petra provide expert advice.

INSIDER TIP
Go vegan!

Natural sponges (left) and spices in all shapes and colours (right) make good souvenirs

MORE BATHING FUN

When your suitcases are full to the brim, you won't have room for a snorkel, fins, a diving mask, beach towels and bathing shoes, which are highly recommended both in the water and on hot sand. But a wide variety of this kind of equipment can be found at reasonable prices in all of the island's beach resorts. The one thing you should take from home is sun lotion because this is heavily overpriced in Greece.

SHOPPING AT THE NEIGHBOURS

If you go on a day trip to Turkish Bodrum in Turkey to shop for leather goods, textiles or jewellery, make sure that you stick to the Greek customs regulations. You are allowed to import goods to a total value of 430 euros. Also duty-free are 40 cigarettes per person. Remember, it is unlikely that you will be able to return your purchases!

SPONGES

Natural sponges are best bought from the pedestrian vendors at the port of Kardámena. For an even bigger selection take a boat trip to the neighbouring sponge divers' island of Kálimnos. The finer the pores of a sponge, the more valuable and more expensive it will be. You can also find peculiar shapes, such as rings or funnels.

INSIDER TIP
Thousands of sponges

SPORT & ACTIVITIES

Cycling, surfing and riding: let the Aegean be your arena! You can wind- and kitesurf to your heart's content, dive amid bubbles rising up from deep in the sea or hang off a rope on a rock wall above the sea.

CLIMBING

Connoisseurs appreciate Kálimnos, the island next to Kos, as an excellent destination for climbers, with its stable climate, the proximity of the climbing areas to resorts and their year-round access. Signposts on the roadside point to the climbing routes. The municipality has published a route guide, and many guesthouses have information available for climbers. General information can be found online at *climbkalymnos.com*; specific questions can be answered on site by the *tourist information office (Mon–Fri 7.30am–3pm | tel. 22 43 02 92 99)* at the ferry dock.

CYCLING

Thanks to a large number – by Greek standards – of cycle paths and gentle ascents, Kos is ideally suited to cycling. Many beach hotels and independent stations hire out touring and mountain bikes, and e-bikes are increasingly on offer as well. A recommended, centrally located station with a large choice of well-kept bikes at good-value rates is *Moto Holidays (Odós Meg. Aléxandrou 17 | tel. 22 42 02 86 76)* in Kos Town.

Moto Harley has several branches: in *Kos (Odós Kanari 42/Odós Neomártiros Christoú | tel. 22 42 02 76 93 | moto-harley.nl)* and *Lambí (main road | tel. 22 42 02 00 61)*. Here, you can also hire Dutch-style bicycles that are rarely seen in the UK: children's tandems (one adult plus one child) and cabbies (one adult plus one baby).

INSIDER TIP
Dutch cycling inspiration

Explore the island's "Wild West" around Kéfalos on a mountain bike

Guided mountain-bike tours on Kos and on the neighbouring islands of Kálimnos and Níssiros are organised by *Kos Bike Activities (at the Hotel Kípriotis Village in Psalídi | tel. 69 44 15 01 29 | kosbikeactivities.com).*

DIVING

The underwater world of *Bubble Beach (p. 93)* alone makes it worth going for a dive. The fascinating bubbling water becomes visible in shallow water and may be enjoyed simply by snorkelling. Snorkelling is permitted in all waters around Kos. Fish may only be harpooned if their length is 25cm or more. Scuba diving is only allowed in a few specific places, and only when accompanied by licensed diving instructors. This is to prevent divers from looking for antiques on the seabed and smuggling them out of the country. The ☂ *Liámis Dive Centre (Odós Mandilára 67 | tel. 69 44 29 58*

30 | kosdiving.com | on-board information daily 7–10pm)* aboard the *MS Apollon*, which sets anchor at night at Mandráki Harbour, offers classes and all kinds of accompanied dives. The *Arian Diving Centre (Kardámena | tel. 22 42 09 22 64 | arian-diving-centre)* is located on the south coast. 🤿 *Kos Divers (Psalídi | in the resort of Kipriótis Village | tel. 69 32 15 54 22 | kosdivers.com)* is particularly family-friendly, allowing children from the age of eight to learn how to scuba dive in one-to-one lessons.

HIKING

Kos is not really suited for a full-on hiking holiday. However, recommended day hikes are available on the Kéfalos peninsula and on the slopes of Mount Díkeos between Asklípion, Zía and Old Pýli. Please note that there aren't any guided hiking tours on offer on Kos, although an Austrian operator, the *Alpinschule Innsbruck (asi-reisen.de)* runs a guided hiking week four times annually. There are no hiking maps or signposted hiking trails. For an overview, consult the 1:60,000 map of Kos published by the Greek publishers Road Edition, which is available on *Farm (see p. 70)* in Marmári and the *Veroútas Family Farm (on the Chrístos Go-Karts road, between Marmári and Tigáki towards the coast | tel. 69 46 84 66 26 | horseriding-kos.com)*. In Kardámena, *Rafael's Trail Riding (tel. 22 42 09 13 04 | mobile 69 40 81 88 22)* is an excellent place to go.

Climbers will find plenty of rocks on the neighbouring island of Kálimnos

Amazon. Thorny scrub makes wearing long trousers a good idea. Sturdy footwear is a must, and don't forget to carry water and wear a sun hat.

RIDING

There are about half a dozen riding stables on Kos, most of which offer horse-riding tours along the beach and sometimes in the mountains, and which also cater for novices. English is spoken everywhere. Two good stables are  *Erika's Horse*

WATERSPORTS

Watersports centres with a large range of activities can be found mainly in larger hotels on the north coast, in Kéfalos Bay, on the beaches of Kardámena and on Paradise Beach. These operators offer waterskiing, windsurfing, paragliding and jet skiing, as well as fun rides. There are opportunities for catamaran sailing on the beach in front of the Caravia Beach hotel to the east of Marmári as well as on Kéfalos Bay.

The best area for windsurfing on the northern coast lies between Marmári and Tigáki. A wind channel between the sandy beach and Psérimos island opposite creates ideal conditions for all levels. Here you'll find several windsurfing and kite stations *(kite surfingkos.com, horizonsurfing.com)*. In Psalídi, windsurfing, wakeboarding, parasailing and jet skis are offered, for example, at *Anemos Windsurf Club (tel. 69 44 73 07 19 | anemoswindsurf. gr)* to the west of the Oceanis Beach Resort. Boats with up to 30hp are also available for hire, and you don't need a sailing licence to operate them.

Kéfalos Bay offers excellent conditions for speedsurfing, with mostly cross-offshore winds. The morning is ideal for beginners, the afternoon for the pros. One long-established station is run by Jens Bartsch from Switzerland on Skála beach: *Kéfalos Windsurfing (tel. 69 77 6203 16 | kefaloswind surfing.com)*.

Next door, *Lynn Yann (tel. 69 73 33 61 43 | lynnyannyoga.com)* offers yoga sessions on SUP boards several times a week.

Specialising in the trendy sport of kitesurfing, Yiánnis Antonoúris operates from Kochilári Beach northeast of Kéfalos: *Kokilári Kite Center (tel. 69 32 47 40 93 | kefaloskite.com)*. Both stations in Kéfalos also hire out SUP boards.

Windsurfing on Kos is great fun for beginners and pros

REGIONAL OVERVIEW

Mastichari ●

Antimachia ●

R. Granal

✈

Kéfalos ●

THE WEST p. 86

Endless beaches and
unspoilt nature

A i g a i o n P e l a g o s

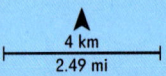

4 km
2.49 mi

Stenon Kapari

Small town by the sea, super lively both day and night

Kos

Platí

KOS TOWN p. 38

Kiragoma

● Pýli

THE CENTRE p. 64

Three resorts, plus beach bars and quiet mountain villages

Kardamena

TURKEY

KOS TOWN

UNIQUE & BEAUTIFUL

In this lively town (pop. 19,000) most of the narrow streets in the centre are free of cars and lined with cafés, bars and tavernas, inviting you to take a break. Archaeological sites are scattered at every turn for when you fancy a wander among the 2,000-year-old columns and walls.

The path along Mandráki Harbour, with its yachts, fishing boats and excursion boats, is the town promenade. Immediately behind this lies the historic centre, full of bars, restaurants and shops.

Enjoy the harbour views from the walls of Nerátza

Summer evenings are spent dancing the night away in the bars that are nestled between the harbour and the ancient Agorá. While young partygoers dance on the bar counters, and thirsty tourists order one shot of alcohol after the other, Greeks prefer clubs that play predominantly Greek rock music. For more sedate entertainment, visit the open-air cinema to watch classics and the latest blockbusters under a starry sky.

KOS TOWN

Mýlos · Lambí Beach · Tarzan Beach · Kritiká Beach

Sófra

Mandílara

Amerikís · Spetson · Kanari · Kanári · Ýdras · Salaminos · Themistokleous

Ameríkis · Psaron · Patakou

Alikarnasou

Vinylio · Konáki

Irodótou · Irodotou

Veriopoulou

Kíprou

Pindou

Meg. Alexandrou

Panagi Tsaldari

ΤΣΑΛΔΑΡΗ ΠΑΝΑΓΗ

15 Alexander Altar

Kolokotroni

Otto e Mezzo

Elía

ΠΙΣΑΝΔΡΟΥ

Poté tin Kyriaki

Megálou Alexándrou

Skevou Zervé · Koritsas · Koritsas

Zaraftou · ΖΑΡΑΦΤΟΥ · Voriou Ipeirou

Grigoriou E · Γρηγορίου Ε

Western Excavation Zone ★ **14**

Nymfaias Nimfeas

Asklípion ★

Platía of Platáni ★

13 Odéon ★

Anapafseos

MARCO POLO HIGHLIGHTS

★ **CASTLE OF THE KNIGHTS OF ST JOHN NERÁTZA**
Flowers, blossom and harbour views
➤ p. 42

★ **CASA ROMANA**
See how rich Romans lived and how they bathed ➤ p. 47

★ **ODÉON**
Take a look in the catacombs where people spent the theatre intervals 1,700 years ago ➤ p. 47

★ **WESTERN EXCAVATION ZONE**
Greek myths in colourful mosaics: one tells the story of a beauty contest among the gods ➤ p. 48

★ **MARKET HALL**
Fresh fruit and Greek treats, presented in a historic setting ➤ p. 54

★ **EMBRÓS THÉRME**
Thermal baths, rustic style ➤ p. 57

★ **PLATÍA OF PLATÁNI**
These restaurant owners put a touch of the spicy East on the table ➤ p. 58

★ **ASKLÍPION**
Healed by the gods – but at a cost ➤ p. 60

6 Mandráki Harbour

4 Castle of the Knights of St John Nerátza ★

Kafeníon in the court building

1 Palazzo di Giustizia

Hadji-Hassan Mosque **5** **3** Nerátzia

2 Hamam

Plane Tree of Hippocrates

Aigaion Pelagos

Neratzias

Limenas Ko

Akti Kountourioti Ακτη Κουντουριωτη

Ακτι Μιαουλι ΑΚΤΙ ΜΙΑΟΥΛΗ

Fish House

Sitar

Synagogue **8**

West

Nova Vita

Áriston

Archaeological Museum **9**

Gatzákis Gold

Aigli

Ciao

10 Defterdar Mosque

7 Agorá

Market Hall ★

Blanc du Nil

11 Church Agía Paraskeví

Haris Cotton

It's all Greek to me

Ippocratous

Ιπποκρατους

O Alís

Orféas

Vasíleos Pavlou

ΒΑΣΙΛΕΩΣ ΠΑΥΛΟΥ

Leof. El. Venizelou

Mitropoleos

Pisandrou

Πισανδρου

Agios Nikolaou

Kleopatras

An. Ioannidi

Korai

Thymanaki

Álla ki Álla

Grigoriou E

Γρηγορίου E

Ironda

12 Casa Romana ★

Embrós Thérme ★

Makrigianni

100 m
109 yd

SIGHTSEEING

1 PALAZZO DI GIUSTIZIA

Alongside all the atrocities committed during the Italian occupation of Kos in the pre-war era between 1928 and 1936, the Italians also left behind some beautiful architecture combining elements of Western Gothic with Oriental styles. Among the reminders from those years are the Market Hall, the Archaeological Museum and the court building reminiscent of a small palace between the coastal road and the Plane Tree of Hippocrates. Inaugurated in 1928, the *Palazzo di Giustizia* still serves in part as a court today, as well as housing various government agencies and the Koan forestry authority. Please feel free to go inside because the inner courtyard is worth seeing, unless, of course, you're a prisoner... Another interesting building from the time of the Italian occupation, the *Albergo Gelsomino* right by the sea, is now a small luxury hotel. ⊙ *5 mins* | ⬚ *d4*

INSIDER TIP
A clean conscience?

WHERE TO START?

Get off the local bus at the terminus at **Aktí Miaoúli** *(⬚ d4)*, only a few steps from the Plane Tree of Hippocrates. The terminal for the long-distance buses is only three minutes from the market hall. If travelling by car, the best place to park is in the car park east of the Casa Romana.

2 HAMAM

This splendidly renovated Turkish bath is, unfortunately, only open as an interesting museum of Ottoman bathing culture, but that's quite good fun, too. The Italians were the first to close it and use it for storing salt harvested in the Tigáki salt lake. *Tue–Sun 9am–4pm* | *admission free* | *Platía Platanoú* | ⊙ *10 mins* | ⬚ *d4*

3 PLANE TREE OF HIPPOCRATES

On a small square between the access to the castle and the Hadji Hassan Mosque, a plane tree still proudly bears its green leaves. Biologists have established its age at nearly 2,000 years. A Koan legend makes it even older, claiming that Hippocrates himself planted it, rested under it and taught his pupils under it too. Another legend tells that St Paul preached Christianity under this very tree. Its exact age cannot be determined as there are no annual rings: inside, the tree is mostly hollow, and what remains of it has to be supported. *Freely accessible at any time* | *Platía Platanoú* | ⊙ *5 mins* | ⬚ *d4*

4 CASTLE OF THE KNIGHTS OF ST JOHN NERÁTZA ⭐

Are you looking for nature and an unusual perspective of the city? The 500-year-old fortress belonging to the crusaders is far more than "just another castle". The castle walls offer a wild and romantic homage to nature. Throughout the fortification, "stone witnesses" to various eras lie scattered between blooming flowers and rampant wild grasses. Round Hellenistic

Colourful beach life in front of the oriental-looking Palazzo di Giustizia

votive altars can serve as picnic tables and, as there are very few barriers, you can climb on most of the walls. The masts of yachts can be seen bobbing up and down behind the fortifications and the city with its mountains beyond is visible through the ramparts. Look out for the coats of arms of the Grand Masters of the Knights of St John painted on the walls or the Arabic digits used by the Ottomans to number their gun casements. *Wed–Mon 8.30am–3.30pm | at the current time, due to earthquake damage, only the anterior area is accessible | admission free |* ⏱ *approx. 30 mins |* 📖 *d3–4*

INSIDER TIP
Numerio riddles & coats of arms

5 HADJI HASSAN MOSQUE

The mosque, built in 1786 and resembling a small palace, is also used commercially with souvenir shops on the ground floor. Only the tall minaret and the ablution fountain right next to the Plane Tree of Hippocrates, whose dome is supported by ancient Corinthian pillars, are an exterior indication of its religious function. *Closed to the public | Platía Platanoú |* 📖 *d4*

6 MANDRÁKI HARBOUR

Many people think that the island's "goats' pen" harbour is the prettiest spot of Kos Town. Excursion boats and sailing yachts, a few fishing boats and often a coastguard speedboat are

It is as if time has stood still at the Agorá of Kos Town – the ancient marketplace

moored in the drop-shaped basin which, to the east, is lined by the walls of the old castle of the Knights of St John with its romantic battlements.

When the lights come on in the evening, the atmosphere becomes particularly special. Then, local families, too, stroll on the wide promenade and the crews of the tourist boats advertise their next day trips, displaying photo albums and videos. What a contrast to past centuries when galley slaves used to shout loudly to each other on this very spot, and when, in antiquity, countless ill people landed here on their journey to the Asklípion and when the Knights of St John set sail on one of their many privateering voyages. One is probably best advised to cherish the here and now!
c–d 3–4

7 AGORÁ

Archaeologists are among the most influential people in Greece. As soon as they excavate something of remote importance, any building work in its vicinity is halted immediately. They are to thank for the romantic park at the heart of the island's capital where you can sit and relax next to ancient columns and temple ruins, as well as under the trees and blossoming shrubs. Kos's medieval centre stood here until 1933 when it was destroyed by a devastating earthquake. When excavators began digging, they exposed an important market, political and social hub: the Agorá. Boards on display at the site provide information on the ruins of the massive columned stoa, a Shrine of Aphrodite and the Temple of Hercules (all from the third/fourth century BCE).

The area's south-western corner still features part of a medieval defensive tower; magnificent bougainvilleas twist their way up the *Toll Gate*, through which you reach Odós Nafklírou from Platía Eleftherías. The gate owes its name to the fact that medieval merchants wanting to sell their wares in Kos had to pay a toll here. *May–Oct Wed–Sun 8am–8pm, Nov–April Wed–Mon 8.30am–3.30pm | admission free | between Odós Nafklírou, Odós Ippókratous, Platía Eleftherías & Defterdar Mosque | ⏱ 40 mins | ▦ d4*

8 SYNAGOGUE

An important reminder: a small synagogue in the old town is testimony to the Jewish community on the island of Kos (as on many of the Greek islands) who lived here until the Nazis invaded. All of the 100 Jews captured were shipped to German concentration camps and none of them returned home. *Closed to the public | Odós Aléxandros Diákou 4 | ▦ d4*

9 ARCHAEOLOGICAL MUSEUM ☂

If museums aren't really your thing, then try and see this one as a narrator, telling tales of the past through its artefacts which depict lives in ancient Greece like in a daily soap opera. The houses and temples of the Greeks and Romans were full of fantasy and horror – but made of stone and clay instead of pixels.

Starting at the entrance, the best thing to do is to proceed directly into the inner courtyard of the museum, the *atrium*. Here, you are standing right in front of a colourful *floor mosaic* dating from the third century CE, i.e. from Roman times. In a section of the image framed by plant tendrils you can see a bearded man leaving a boat and placing his left foot onto a narrow jetty. On land, he is greeted by a simply dressed man with a hat and stick. The left-hand corner of the mosaic shows a seated bearded man wrapped in a white garment in front of a rock. This is the physician Hippocrates receiving the visit of Asklípios, the god of healing. The man greeting them is a passing peasant.

The atrium holds several *Roman statues* too. Impressive, although not exactly beautiful, is the group of figures in an almost baroque style: the naked god Dionysus, drunk, is holding an empty wine goblet in one hand. He is leaning on a vine which is crowned by Pan, the god of shepherds, recognisable by his goat's feet, short horns and pan flute. With his right arm, the feminine-looking Dionysus is leaning on a satyr, an inebriated young man from his retinue. Sitting at their feet, a small Eros, the personification of eroticism, is caressing a wild animal. The work has been dated to the second or third century CE.

Hippocrates receives a divine visitor: floor mosaic in the Archaeological Museum

A bit further on, another statue shows an older naked man hanging from a tree, his hands tied. This is Marsyas, a satyr from Dionysus's entourage. An excellent flute player, Marsyas had agreed to a musical competition with the god Apollo. It was decided that the vanquished opponent should be placed unconditionally in the hands of the victor. Thus, the divine winner had the blasphemous Marsyas hung from a tree and skinned alive.

Also quite eye-catching are two *statues of the multi-breasted Artemis.* However, the experts are divided on whether the shapes on her upper body are indeed breasts or rather bull's testicles: in the opinion of some archaeologists it was the custom in the large Artemis temple of Ephesus in Asia Minor to tack on the testicles of sacrificed animals to the marble statue of the goddess.

The largest room in the museum shows mainly *Hellenistic statues.* One room at the northern end shelters the museum's most valuable sculpture in terms of art history: a thoughtful-looking male figure dating from the fourth century BCE and probably representing the physician Hippocrates. *Core opening hours May–Oct Wed–Mon 8am–8pm (admission 6 euros), otherwise 8.30am–3pm (admission 3 euros) | Platía Eleftherías | ⏱ 45 mins | ⊞ c4*

🔟 DEFTERDAR MOSQUE
Built in 1725, this mosque was severely damaged by an earthquake in the summer of 2017, and it is questionable whether it will ever be rebuilt. However, the building is picturesque even in its current state and gives the town yet another oriental touch. *Platía Eleftherías | ⊞ c4*

11 AGÍA PARASKEVÍ CHURCH

The Bishop of Kos leads a modest life… his small residential palace stands directly above the market hall opposite the chapel of St Paraskeví, the latter having been severely damaged in the 2017 earthquake and awaiting restoration. *Platía Agías Paraskevís* | ⏱ *5 mins* | 🗺 *c4*

12 CASA ROMANA ⭐

There have been millionaires since time immemorial. The owner of this splendid Roman villa was surely one of them. His private yacht may have sunk but his residence was excavated by Italian archaeologists. They reconstructed it so well that today the house gives a vivid impression of life in Roman times. Travelling through time in your imagination, spare a thought in the midst of this world of luxury for the slaves working here. A characteristic shared by many Roman houses is the inner courtyard. The "Roman House" on Kos has three of them. Two belong to the peristyle courtyard type, being surrounded on three (or four) sides by pillars or columns. The colonnade in the large peristyle courtyard even has two storeys.

The small peristyle courtyard leads into the *triclinium* adjoining to the south; this is the dining room of the house. In the triclinium the family would eat their dinner lying on stone benches – usually three – fitted with precious fabrics and cushions. The walls of the downstairs rooms were partly clad with marble panels, decorated with murals. In some places you can still make out what remains

of them. The floor also consisted of marble slabs or was decorated with colourful mosaics.

The mosaic in the smallest of the three inner courtyards depicts a leopard and a lion, each killing an antelope. The mosaics in the peristyle courtyard next to the dining room represent two leopards, dolphins and a nereid – a friendly sea nymph from the entourage of the god Poseidon. According to ancient belief the nereids entertained seafarers with music and dance and would help them if their ship was in distress. Finally, a mosaic in the large peristyle courtyard represents an exquisitely beautiful panther and a tiger. All the mosaics in the Casa Romana date back to the third century CE.

The grounds of the Casa Romana also shelter the *remnants of the Roman thermal baths*. The well-preserved hypocaust pillars built from round clay slabs would have supported the floor, piping hot air through below – an ancient underfloor heating system. *April–Oct usually daily 8am–8pm (admission 6 euros), Nov–April Wed–Mon 8.30am–3pm (admission 3 euros)* | *Odós Grigoríou E'* | ⏱ *40 mins* | 🗺 *c5*

13 ODÉON ⭐ 🐾

Every ancient city had at least one theatre. Originally, the entire building and its 15 rows of seats were covered in the Kos Odéon, built in the second century CE. These days, the odd performance is still given here in high summer. The catacombs below the galleries were used as stalls and bars

– evidence that intervals were also part of the performance back in Roman times. *Freely accessible during the day | admission free | Odós Grigoríou E' | ⏲ 20–30 mins | ▥ b5*

14 WESTERN EXCAVATION ZONE

A stroll through the western excavation zone is something like visiting an archaeological adventure playground. Rather than having to keep to prescribed paths, you can scramble around between the many pillars and climb any wall. Lizards scurry about, and in the spring a carpet of flowers covers the archaeological site between the Old Town, Odéon and Casa Romana.

Clearly visible, the two main roads of this ancient area still have some well-preserved old cobbles in parts. The long row of pillars that was re-erected in 1930 belonged to the *gymnasion*, a hall where athletes would have trained. The impressive wall remains were part of Roman thermal baths whose foundations were later used for an Early Christian basilica.

Several floor mosaics of villas are worth a closer look. The largest is kept under a modern protective roof on the northern edge of the excavation zone. A frieze full of amusing representations of wild animals runs around a rectangular image showing the Judgement of Páris, where the most beautiful of men has to judge who is the most beautiful among the three goddesses Aphrodite, Athena and Hera.

Two further entertaining mosaics await at the eastern end of the excavation zone below smaller protective roofs at their original site. The gladiators represented here must have been as popular as professional footballers today, as they are even named in inscriptions: Aigialos, Zephyros and Ylas. The mosaic shows the half-naked Zephyros with a trident and short sword in his hands fighting Ylas, wearing helmet, shield and breastplate. The second mosaic explains how a continent got its name: Zeus has fallen in love with the young Phoenician princess Europa. Changing into the shape of a white bull, Zeus carries her off to Crete and makes her his wife. From then on, the European continent has borne the name of this beautiful princess. The mosaic shows the scene of the abduction. A dolphin accompanies the two on their voyage across the seas, while Eros bearing the Flame of Desire in his hand is leading the bull. *Wed–Mon 8.30am–3pm | admission free | north of Odós Grigoríou E'| ⏲ 45 mins–1 hr | ▥ b–c 4–5*

15 ALEXANDER ALTAR

All Greek school children are taught that Alexander the Great was a heroic king who was responsible for spreading the Greek culture as far as Northern India around 2,300 years ago. In Greece, it is taboo to refer to him as a warrior who slaughtered many people. You can find out how he saw himself by reading the text from one of his letters chiselled into stone – and translated into English – on this kitsch monument. In this letter he, of all people, calls the peoples of the Earth to find eternal peace which he has created. *Freely accessible | Odós Tsaldári/Odós El. Venizélou |* ⏱ *5 mins |* ▥ *c4*

EATING & DRINKING

AIGLI

Run by a women's cooperative, Aigli is the best café in the city centre. The women who work here are either single parents, victims of a broken marriage or of social deprivation and see this job as a new start in life. Coke, Pepsi and the like are banned from the menu whereas regional ingredients and Greek produce are promoted, for example the extremely tasty Vikos Cola produced in northwest Greece. Other typically Greek products include almond milk, *soumáda*, the cinnamon lemonade *kanneláda* and the sour cherry lemonade *vissináda*. Many of the cocktails are mixed with Greek spirits. The snacks are prepared by a chef who swears she would serve these dishes to her loved one. *Daily | Platía Eleftherías | diagonally opposite the market hall | aiglikos.gr | € |* ▥ *c4*

INSIDER TIP
Real Greek cola

ÁLLA KI ÁLLA

Local people and expats alike love this typical *mezedopolío* in a villa with a small garden terrace which is over 100 years old. Here, instead of a set menu or mighty portion, you order several small servings. These are placed in the centre of the table, and

Workout in antiquity: the gymnasium's columns have lasted for 2,000 years

When you have had your fill of old stones, come to Platía Eleftherías for a break

everyone helps themselves. Pork chops are one of their culinary delights. Except in the peak summer season, there is often live Greek music on Friday and Saturday evenings as well as on early Sunday afternoon – and even the guests tentatively join in. *Daily | Odós Grigoríou E' 35 | near the large car park west of the Casa Romana | €€ | ⊞ c5*

ÁRISTON

This small bakery, with only a few tables and chairs at the back of the Archaeological Museum, is the perfect place to try a *bugátsa*, a filo pastry filled with semolina pudding that is beloved by the Greeks, for breakfast. If this is not sweet enough, order with honey for only 10 cents extra. *Mon–Sat 8am–1pm | Platía Eleftherías | ⊞ c4*

INSIDER TIP
Sweet breakfast

CIAO

Take a catwalk seat in front of this café to see not only supermodels but people from all walks of life sporting the craziest tattoos and the worst holiday outfits. The town offers no better place for a spot of people-watching, accompanied by one of the home-made cakes or an Aperol Spritz, the café's favourite tipple. *Daily | Odós Ifaistou 2 | €€ | ⊞ c4*

INSIDER TIP
Crazy catwalk

ELÍA

Owner Sotíris is a professional chef who learned his trade in Germany. He interprets classic Greek dishes in a modern way. The list of wines from Kos and ouzo brands from all over Greece is exceptional. *Daily May–Oct, otherwise closed Mon–Wed | Odós Apelloú 27 | elia-kos.gr | €€ | 🗺 c4*

FISH HOUSE

This restaurant, located only a few steps from the tourist hustle and bustle and near Mandráki Harbour, resembles a film set for *Mamma Mia*! Everything follows a maritime theme, including fishing nets, anchors, amphoras and a small boat. While the cuisine is average, the atmosphere is great! *Daily | Parodós 25is Martíou | €€ | 🗺 c4*

KAFENÍON IN THE COURTHOUSE ⚑

In every democracy, most trials are open to the public. The same is true on Kos, but things are done a bit differently here: access to the courthouse is through a nameless *kafeníon*, whose plastic chairs stand outside on the square next to the Plane Tree of Hippocrates. When the court is in session, the door behind the café and the court room always remains wide open, so that you can observe Greek court proceedings for a few minutes without drawing attention to yourself. *Open only on trial days | Platía Platanoú | € | 🗺 d4*

KONÁKI

Very hungry? Try this popular grill for its tasty chicken, gyros and other Greek grill specialities in large portions. The meat comes from their own butcher's. *Daily | Odós Kanári 1 | € | 🗺 c3*

MÝLOS

Looking for the ultimate place to relax? Situated next to an old windmill, this beach bar is perfect for chilling out under parasols and palm trees – the sun loungers are free for paying guests. Drinks and snacks, as well as the assortment of ouzo, are all served to you on the beach – we'd advise taking a seat on the terrace if you've ordered the giant T-bone steak. Mýlos often turns into a party hotspot at night with campfires burning on the beach. *Daily | €€ | 🗺 0*

NERÁTZIA

In this small café between the courthouse and the old hamam you can sit in the shade of mighty trees and watch the world go by, sipping freshly pressed juice, a *freddo espresso* or ouzo and wine. You will be served by the owner in person, which is why they close here around 6pm. *Daily | in the alleyway between the Plane Tree of Hippocrates and the eastern shoreline road | € | 🗺 d4*

O ALÍS

The proprietor of this restaurant specialises in Turkish cuisine. He personally prefers to label his cuisine as Anatolian so as not to scare off holidaymakers from the Greek mainland. Guests come in droves to try his cooking, which is a slightly different take on traditional food. Try the *ádana kebab* which is already spicy enough for the Greeks. *Daily | Odós Artemisías 23 | alirestaurantkos.gr | € | ⌑ e5*

OTTO E MEZZO

The finest Italian cuisine awaits you in this 140-year-old townhouse. The pasta is home-made, the pizzas are stone-baked – you'd never know that the owner and head chef are both Greek. *Daily | Odós Apelloú 21 | €€€ | ⌑ c4*

POTÉ TIN KYRIAKÍ

In the idyllic garden of *Never on Sundays* we recommend that you order some of the many hors d'oeuvres, such as *anthoús*, filled courgette flowers. There's often live Greek music on weekend evenings. *Closed Sun | Odós Pisándrou 9 | € | ⌑ c5*

SÓFRA

When this Turkish restaurant moved from Platáni to the island's capital a few years ago, its name was changed from *Hasan* to *Sófra*, meaning table. Their cuisine has remained Anatolian, and at weekends the spicy food is often served to live Greek music. *Daily | Odós Averóf 5 | €€ | ⌑ c3*

TARZAN BEACH

Has everyone gone completely crazy here? As the name suggests, the entire restaurant has a rainforest theme with the service team headed by Tarzan and Jane – you'll even hear the occasional roar from the forest.  A party mood reigns all day long: sun loungers are so close together that you'll quickly get to know your neighbour. The emphasis is more on socialising than on food, which is fairly average. By the way, the entire Tarzan theme is actually based on a linguistic misunderstanding: the restaurant stands on the former site of a *tarsanás*, a place used to store small boats in winter. The first foreign tourists then read this as "Tarzan" and gave the proprietor his business idea. *Daily | Tarsanás Beach | Odós Sokratoús 3 | € | ⌑ c1*

SPELLING FUN

Koans hate strict rules and are quite liberal where their spelling is concerned – a custom that can cause confusion for tourists. In Greek, place names can be written differently on signs and maps, while the Latin spelling is even more haphazard. *"Agía"* meaning "Saint" is a good example; it is sometimes written as *"Agía"* (as in the Marco Polo guides) or *"Aghía"* or even *"Ayía"*. All three spellings are accepted and combined, as the Greeks please. The best thing about this: where there are no rules, there are fewer mistakes.

Just browsing? Perfect – Odós Iféstou will have something for you!

VINYLIO

In this modern but small restaurant, young siblings Flavio and Rozeta combine Greek and Sicilian cuisine. He is an excellent sommelier while she is great at all kinds of risotto, filled mushroom and chicken dishes. *Daily | Odós Amerikís 1 | €€ | ᙁ c3*

SHOPPING

☂ The most important shopping streets in town for holidaymakers are *Odós Iféstou* and the adjoining *Odós Apéllou (ᙁ c4)* where all the shops are seven days a week and in the evening almost until midnight. Local people, on the other hand, prefer to shop between the ancient Agorá and *Odós Korái (ᙁ c–d 4–5).*

BLANC DU NIL

This shop sells items of clothing in any colour as long as it is white. Blouses, shirts, dresses, trousers and other items are all made from elegant white Egyptian cotton of the finest quality. The only items not for sale are wedding dresses. *Odós Iféstou 13 | ᙁ c4*

GATZÁKIS GOLD

Theodóros Gatzákis and his German wife Ulrike run this jewellery shop in Kos Town. They like to spend time chatting to their customers while also telling tales about Kos and its inhabitants. When they're not entertaining their customers, they sell a tasteful selection of modern gold jewellery. Pieces are far less opulent than is often the case in Greece. They are proud that they only work with solid stones rather than chippings. *Odós Galias Passanikoláki 1* | 🗺 *c4*

HARIS COTTON

If you love colour, then have a look at the fashion for women, men and children, created by one of Greece's biggest textile manufacturers. All clothing is made from cotton, most of which comes from Greece. *Odós Iféstou 25* | 🗺 *c4*

IT'S ALL GREEK TO ME

In this small shop you can be sure that all the souvenirs and designer objects are actually made in Greece. They don't sell kitsch, but rather items such as candles that are shaped like ancient columns and mugs that bear quotes by Greek philosophers. *Odós Apelloú 4* | *sophia.com.gr* | 🗺 *c4*

MARKET HALL ★

A paradise for vegetarians and vegans: they don't sell meat or fish here, but lots of fruit, nuts, olives and Greek specialities. Built by the Italians in 1934 and now fully air-conditioned, the small Market Hall has no equal in terms of cleanliness and order in the whole of Greece. However, today the original range of fresh fruit and vegetables is being encroached upon by more and more culinary and other souvenirs for holidaymakers. These days, you can buy anything from *soumáda* almond milk from the island of Rhodes or sweet pickled carrots from the northern Greek town of Kavála to herbs, sponges and shell bowls. A typically Koan proposition are sweet pickled mini tomatoes,

watermelon pieces and aubergine slices *(glikó omatáki, glikó melitzanáki, glikó karpoúzi)*.

It is safe to wash your fresh fruit at the fountain right inside the market hall. Pay at the tills on the way out. *Mon–Sat 7am–10.30pm, Sun 10am– 10.30pm* | *Platía Eleftherías/Platía Agías Paraskevís* | 🗺 *c4*

SPORT & ACTIVITIES

TRENÁKI 👥

These small trains on rubber wheels, which drive through the lanes of the island's capital, are a great way to see a lot of the town when with small children. One departs from Mandráki Harbour for approx. 20-minute city tours, while another sets off from the central terminal for local buses by the shoreline road to the east of the castle, heading for the Asklípion. *Tickets approx. 5 euros*

BEACHES

As soon as you leave the harbour basin, at each end, you will find narrow sand-and-pebble beaches. In immediate proximity to the town, they are always busy, and in high season they get really crowded. The most popular is 🏖 *Kritiká Beach*.

Towards *Psalídi* things get quieter, and occasionally meadows with trees go down all the way to the shore. Towards 🏖 *Lambí* too, the beach becomes emptier the further you get away from the harbour, and joins the sandy ribbon of miles and miles of beaches along the northern coast.

WELLNESS

Several hotels have spas. Open also to non-residents is the *Mazarin Luxury Health Club* in the *Diamond Deluxe* designer hotel *(🕮 c3)* *(Lambí-Neá Alikarnassós | 5km west of Mandráki Harbour | tel. 22 42 04 88 35 | diamondhotel.gr)*. Their four-hour luxury treatment in a private spa suite is the epitome of their exclusive range of treatments.

NIGHTLIFE

No other Greek island, with the exception of Mykonos, can boast a nightlife as intense as that of Kos Town. The numerous clubs usually only empty towards dawn. A particularly high density of establishments can be found in the Old Town *(🕮 d4)* between Mandráki harbour and the Agorá.

NOVA VITA

How do the Greeks like to party? The latest Greek sounds are played in this relatively small *ellinádiko* (club). The only thing missing to complete the authentic Greek atmosphere is the classic *sirtaki* dance. Let yourself be surprised! *Odós Pléssa/Odós Nafklírou | 🕮 d4*

ORFÉAS

How would you feel about meeting Tom Hanks, Brad Pitt or Leonardo di Caprio under the starry skies of Kos? Your chances of seeing your favourite stars in action are high at the open-air

Why not try the sweet pickled fruit in the Market Hall in Kos Town?

The days by the sea may be too short, but the nights in Kos Town are long!

cinema. Popcorn, *souvlaki* and drinks are available at the bar. *Showings: June–mid-Sept daily 8.30pm or 9pm and 10.30pm or 11pm | ticket 7 euros, 3D films 9 euros | on the eastern town beach between harbour and marina, Odós Vas. Georgíou/Odós Fenarétis |* e5

SITAR

On many evenings, the guests dance outside this well-styled cocktail bar by Mandráki Harbour, enjoying the view of the many boats and yachts. They organise special events and themed evenings. *Odós Koundourióti | FB: Sitar Cocktail Bar |* c4

WEST

This club in the Bar Street Area serves shots of alcohol to quench the thirst of its Scandinavian guests who order shots by the metre. Guests are often seen dancing on the tables and bar. *Bar Street |* d4

AROUND KOS TOWN

PSALÍDI

5km / 10 mins from Kos Town by bus
Starting right next to the eastern limits of Kos Town, Psalídi consists mainly of large, good-quality hotels and a string of tavernas. The beaches are fairly narrow and often pebbly. Buses operate until late in the evening to take you from your accommodation in Psalídi to Kos Town.

Psalídi, the island's most north-westerly point, is home to the *Psalídi Wetland*. With its lake of brackish water, these wetlands are an important stopping-off point for numerous migrating birds between autumn and spring, amongst them flamingos and herons. Unfortunately, the entire site looks extremely neglected – the remains of an old leisure pool are an eyesore, but this doesn't seem to bother the native or migratory birds. 🎦 *L2*

ÁGIOS FÓKAS

10km / 40 mins from Kos Town by bicycle

On the island's southwest cape, the Greek military has painted a large Greek flag on the cliff and erected a lookout post and an antenna to signal to the Turkish military that they have nothing to search for in this area. Taking photographs is forbidden here. Fortunately, the adjacent 🏝 *Ágios Fókas Beach*, with its scenic beauty, is for civilian use. 🎦 *M3*

EMBRÓS THÉRME ★ 🐗

15km / 30 mins from Kos Town by bus

The thermal spa of Kos doesn't really bear comparison with Bath or other continental thermal baths. It consists of a simple pump house and a stone circle in the sea right on 🏝 *Embrós Thérme Beach*, forming a basin of about 10m in diameter. At the beginning of the season, the spa may still bear the mark of the winter storms, making it rather less attractive. The general opinion on the spa is divided

AROUND KOS TOWN

Aigaion Pelagos

4 km / 45 mins

Κως **Kos**

Πλατάνι
Platáni

Κακό Πρινάρι
Kako Prinári

Ψαλίδι
Psalídi

Platía of Platáni ★

10km / 40 mins

Παραδείσι
Paradisi

Ασκλήπιον ★
Asklípion ★

Γιαπιλη
Giapili

14km / 25 mins

Ágios Fókas
Beach

Άγιος Φωκάς
Agios Fókas

2 km
1.24 mi

Embrós Thérme ★

At Embrós Thérme you simultaneously enjoy both seawater and fresh water

as some people love it, but others complain about its simplicity.

At Embrós Thérme the water, at a temperature of up to 40°C, comes from a source in the rock and mixes with the seawater. According to one medical analysis, the water has healing properties which can help with problems of childhood development, as well as with skin conditions and problems with blood vessels and the respiratory tract.

A few sun loungers and sunshades are available for hire along the small pebble beaches nearby. The thermal baths are located below the tarmac road, shortly before it ends. Although it is possible to drive down the very steep track, it's best to leave your car on the allocated places on the tarmac road. This is also where you'll find the shelter for the town bus and at least one *kantína* selling drinks and snacks. Another snack bar is located down at the beach. *Freely accessible at all times, even at night* | 📖 *L3*

PLATÁNI

2km / 8 mins from Kos Town by bus
Platáni is proof that people of different religions can live side by side in peace and harmony. The village is inhabited by both Greek Christians and Greek Muslims. The tiny ⭐ 🏴 *platía* (village square) is lined with tavernas run by Turkish-born Koans where Christians also come to eat.

INSIDER TIP
A sweets lover's paradise

The *Mous Pastry House (daily 7am–9.30pm)* on the road to the Asklípion, where all the cakes, gateaux, pastries and eastern delicacies are home-made, is said to be the best on the island.

There is a mosque as well as a church. On the edge of the village, alongside a Christian and two Muslim graveyards, there is a Jewish cemetery too. Friday afternoon prayers attract a fair few believers, while the prayer leader or *hodja* tends to be alone in his place of worship for the five daily prayersr Turkish-speaking Muslims, whose children attend the regular Greek schools.

On the southern edge of Platáni village, immediately to the left of the road leading up here from Kos Town, look out for two cemeteries that are worth seeing. Sadly, the gate, adorned with two stars of David, is locked, but you can look through it to get a glimpse of the tombs of the Jewish community which in 1922 still numbered 66 members. However, in 1943 they were rounded up by the German occupation forces and taken to concentration camps where most of them were murdered.

The gate to the Muslim cemetery, 200m further north, is usually open during the day. Hundreds of the older tombstones bear Arabic inscriptions, whereas the more recent gravestones resemble those of the Christian cemeteries, showing – and this is unusual in Islam – the names of the dead and their dates of birth and death. On the road between Platáni and the Asklípion, the extensive premises of the *International Hippocratic Foundation of Kos* appear neglected. The office building is empty apart from a tiny *museum (mostly 9am–4pm | admission 3 euros)* which displays a few medical exhibits from the Asklípion. Their *Hippocratic Garden* offers pretty views, but sadly not much else. *Buses from Kos Town to Platáni run roughly every half hour between 7am and 11pm |* ▭ *K2*

"KOZE" OR "KOSS"?

Foreigners often ask how to pronounce the name of both the island and the town, and there is a clear answer: firstly, modern Greek doesn't have any closed long vowels, and secondly the Greek letter *sigma* – the "s" – is always pronounced sharply and is voiceless. Therefore, Kos is pronounced "Koss" – not "Koze"; in other words, it is pronounced like "cross" but without the "r".

Accordingly, we now also know how to say the name of the village of Kéfalos in the island's west, namely "Kefaloss" – not "K'farlos". As is the case with all multisyllabic Greek words, the accent always indicates which syllable should be stressed.

ASKLÍPION ⭐

4km / 15 mins from Kos Town by mini-train

Medical doctors were around 2,300 years ago. On the island of Kos, the hospital was a sanctuary with temples and thermal baths in the middle of the countryside. Patients would sacrifice animals to the god of healing Asklípios (Asclepius) and his father Apollo. Parts of the animal flesh would be burnt so that the smoke would rise up to the god and the rest of the meat would be shared among the physicians, priests and patients. This treatment would usually be enough to cure minor ailments.

Those suffering more serious illnesses were forced to fast and were probably drugged. The practice of "temple sleep" was common: patients would go to sleep in the temple with the expectation that they would be visited by Asclepius himself. They

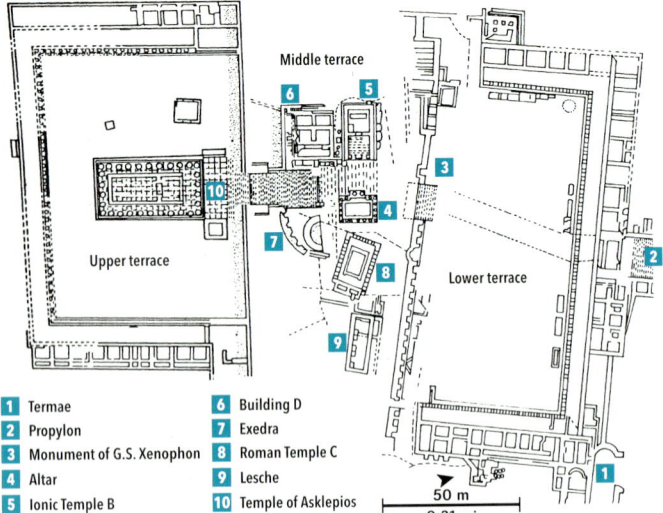

ASKLÍPION

Middle terrace

Upper terrace

Lower terrace

1	Termae	6	Building D
2	Propylon	7	Exedra
3	Monument of G.S. Xenophon	8	Roman Temple C
4	Altar	9	Lesche
5	Ionic Temple B	10	Temple of Asklepios

50 m
0.31 mi

The Asklípion was both a sanctuary and a place of healing

would then report their dream to the doctors, who would diagnose their illness and prescribe a type of cure in accordance with the scientific knowledge of the time. These methods had an extremely effective psychosomatic effect because the faithful patient usually kept to the strict regime and was convinced of its efficacy.

The sanctuary is laid out in terraces. The lowest terrace was mainly reserved for recuperation and medical purposes. Once, several temples would have stood on the central terrace, together with a sacrificial altar and buildings used by the priests. The largest and most splendid temple, an edifice dedicated to Asklípios, would have stood on the uppermost terrace from the second century BCE.

From today's entrance, a reconstructed *marble staircase* with 23 steps leads up to the first terrace, with an area of 93 x 47m. Here, visitors were received at a a gatehouse, the *propylon*, once adorned with four pillars; the foundation walls can still be made out. The first terrace was surrounded by a covered walk, called a *stoa*. Rising in the east since Roman times, behind the covered walk, was a building holding the thermal baths. Today the south is still bounded by a long wall.

Thirty broad steps lead up to the central terrace where several of the most interesting pillars have been placed in an upright position again. The two Ionic pillars to the right belong to the *Asklípios Temple* dating back to the early third century BCE. The *cella* has a chamber built into the floor, probably to keep the temple treasure safe. Many pilgrims gifted large sums of money to the sanctuary after being healed.

The *Altar of Asklípios* east of the temple was originally a rather

Splendid columns remain from several temples from the Asklípion's heyday

imposing building. An open courtyard was surrounded on three sides by colonnades in the Ionic style running along the top of a marble foundation and open towards the temple. In the centre of the courtyard stood the sacrificial table for burnt offerings. Standing between the pillars of the hall were statues of Asklípios, his daughter Hygeia and other goddesses. A marble ramp led up to the courtyard in order to make it easier to pull in the sacrificial animals. They were then sacrificed and burned on this altar. East of the altar, seven re-erected Corinthian pillars mark the outlines of a Corinthian *Temple* of *Apollo* from the second/third century.

A reconstructed flight of 60 steps leads onto the uppermost terrace, which measures 100 x 80m. From the second century BCE a *circular Doric temple* would have risen at its centre, the most magnificent of all the temples in the sanctuary and dedicated to Asklípios. The temple was surrounded by a colonnade with six columns on each of the narrow sides and eleven columns along each of the long sides (counting the corner columns twice), enveloping the massive core wall of the *pronaos* and *cella*. In early Christian times the temple was converted into a church. Dating from that time is an improvised altar: on top of an ancient column stump lies an ancient capital, and on top of the capital an ancient stone slab. In order to Christianise these pagan parts of the building, the Greek letters *IC XC* were chiselled into the capital, standing for the name of Jesus Christ and still quite legible.

Towards the south, east and west the uppermost terrace is surrounded by Doric colonnades from the first half of the second century BCE with 73 columns, replacing an even older structure that was completely made of wood. These *incubation halls* would have been used by pilgrims for what was called "healing sleep". *May–Oct daily 8am–8pm (admission 8 euros), Nov–April Wed-Mon 8am–3pm (admission 4 euros) | town buses depart from the bus terminal by the shoreline; trenáki (mini-trains) depart from Mandráki Harbour |* ⏱ *1–1½ hrs |* 🗺 *J2*

WHERE TO STAY IN KOS TOWN

WELL LOOKED AFTER

Being a guest of Aléxis and his wife Dionysía at the *Afendoúlis (23 rooms | Odós Evripílou 1 | tel. 22 42 02 53 21 | afendoulishotel. com | €)* is like being part of a Greek family. Breakfast is only available à la carte and most of the jams are homemade by Dionysía. The hotel lobby doubles up as the family's living and dining room, where nice guests are invited to join them at the table. Their daughter Kyriakí and her husband Dimítri, who grew up in Australia, speak English even better than the parents. A narrow stretch of beach is located just 150m away. Don't be put off by the small room sizes – the hotel has a delightful terrace with sweet-smelling jasmine where you can sit and read your book.

BY THE SEA

No other hotel on the island stands closer to the water than the *Kos Aktis (48 rooms | Odós Vassilíos Geórgios B' 7 | tel. 22 42 04 72 00 | kosaktis.gr | €€€)*. This doesn't come as a surprise seeing that the state commissioned its construction in the 1960s when there were no building regulations in place to prevent seafront construction. In 2005, the building was refurbished as a designer hotel by a private investor and was saved from demolition. All rooms look out on to the Aegean Sea, with some even offering sea views from the bathtub. On the hotel terrace – open to the public – you are practically sitting on the edge of the surf. Named after the chemical formula for water, the hotel restaurant *(daily | €€€)* is called $H2O$.

THE CENTRE

BEACHES, TEMPLES & MORE

You don't need a sat nav here – it's straightforward territory: the beach stretches along the entire northern coastline from Kos Town to the power plant. Between the two lie the three seaside resorts of Tigáki, Marmári and Mastichári, as well as a few big beach hotels, a salt lake and Tam Tam – the island's most beautiful beach bar.

Two kilometres inland is the main road to the airport and Kéfalos, with two unspoilt villages. Minor roads, often winding, lead to a

At the end of a winding road: coastal views from Antimáchia castle

handful of villages on the slopes of Mount Díkeos, which still have the air of traditional Greece. It is worth stopping for a break on the village squares. Here, you can discover a couple of castles, churches with beautiful murals, many pretty cafés and good tavernas.

At sunset, the islanders meet at Zía, Kos's highest village. Finally, two roads lead down to Kardámena on the south coast, where you can bathe and also enjoy the vibrant nightlife.

THE CENTRE

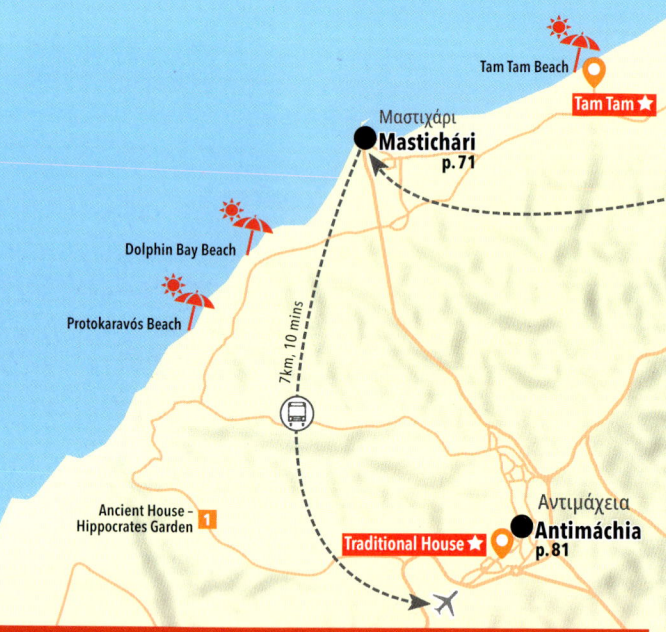

Tam Tam Beach

Tam Tam ⭐

Μαστιχάρι

● **Mastichári**
p. 71

Dolphin Bay Beach

Protokaravós Beach

7km, 10 mins

Ancient House –
Hippocrates Garden 1

Traditional House ⭐

Αντιμάχεια

● **Antimáchia**
p. 81

MARCO POLO HIGHLIGHTS

⭐ **TAM TAM**
What on earth are cows doing at this
taverna? ➤ p. 72

⭐ **NERÓMILOS**
There's no better place to relax in Zía than
in front of the old watermill ➤ p. 76

⭐ **LAGOÚDI**
It doesn't get less touristy than this. And
the village priest is always appreciative of
a quick hello ➤ p. 78

⭐ **TOMB OF HARMYLOS**
An archaeological treat in a thoroughly
Greek setting ➤ p. 79

⭐ **PALIÁ PIGÍ (OLD WATERSPRING)**
Time seems to stand still at this taverna
next to the oldest fountain on Kos ➤ p. 79

⭐ **OLD PÝLI (PALÉA PÝLI)**
A ghost village in the forest, a ruined
Byzantine castle with panoramic views
and a cosy café ➤ p. 80

⭐ **TRADITIONAL HOUSE**
See how a peasant family lived 60 years
ago ➤ p. 81

Alikés Beach

4km, 1 hr 10 mins

Τιγκάκι
Tigáki
p. 68

Carávia Beach

Μαρμάρι
Marmári
p. 69

Ζηπάρι
Zipari

14km, 50 mins

Ασφενδιού
Asfendiou

Αμανιου
Amaniou

3 **Lagoúdi** ★

Ζια
Zía
p. 75   **Nerómilos** ★

Πυλί
Pýli
p. 78   **Tomb of Harmylos** ★

4 **Old Pýli (Paléa Pýli)** ★

Paliá Pigí (Old Waterspring) ★

Mount Díkeos   **2**

5 Antimáchia Castle (Kástro)

Τολαρι
Tolari

Καρδάμαινα
Kardámena
p. 82

A i g a i o n

P e l a g o s

1.5 km
0.93 mi

TIGÁKI

(☐ H2) **Tigáki is an expansive resort with a good distance between each of the hotels.**

Even 🚩 cows have room to graze on the grassland between the houses and along the long stretch of beach which gives the village its rural appeal. For shopping and nightlife, you'll need to travel into town, but thanks to its proximity (it's 10km from Kos Town), a taxi ride at night will not cost the earth, or you could even wait for the first bus back in the morning at 8am! Otherwise, Tigáki is mainly known as a seaside resort. It's worth a visit even if you're not staying here for its three splendid restaurants. And if you're lucky, you will spot flamingos here in spring and autumn.

SIGHTSEEING

ALIKÉS SALT LAKE
The former salt pans (where no salt has been harvested for a long time) today enjoy environmental protection. In the winter months, numerous water birds make their home here, including flamingos. *Freely accessible | 800m west of the roundabout*

EATING & DRINKING

AMBÉLI
You are spoilt for choice in this outdoor taverna with over 60 *mezedákia* (Greek tapas) to choose from, both hot and cold, and all at a set price of four to six euros. The menu includes vegetarian options as well as offal and lamb's testicles. The portions are ample and three dishes per person are enough to fill any-one. If there are four of you, you'll need five days to eat your way through the entire menu – and then you can call yourself a true connoisseur of Greek cuisine. *Daily | off the coastal road, about 2.5km east of the roundabout (watch out for the signpost there) | €–€€*

INSIDER TIP
Menu for the curious

PLÓRI
Your host Michális and his son Jánnis serve local fish and mussels. Their olives are a delight as is the warm aubergine salad and sour pickled fish *(gávros xidáto)*. Every day, the dessert selection will include a home-made, relatively low-sugar option. *Daily | on the coastal road 80m west of the roundabout | €€*

SPORT & ACTIVITIES

Watersports and riding are popular activities. For more information, see the Sport & activities chapter (p. 32).

BEACHES

The fine sandy 🌿 *Alikés Beach* goes on for miles. The widest section (over 60m) is in front of the resort's centre where the sun loungers are lined up. The beach becomes gradually narrower towards the east, but is still busy with tourists. Westwards near the salt pans, it is more secluded and is popular with nude bathers.

WELLNESS

ARTEMIS HAMAM & SPA

The spa temple for the general public on Kos is the modern *Artemis Hamam & Spa* in Tigáki. It offers two large public steam baths and a smaller private one that can be booked as well as two saunas (swimsuits required) and several rooms for massages and beauty treatments. You can even smoke a water pipe in the attached Garden Bar. Men can treat themselves to a traditional wet shave at the barber's shop. The hamam provides free entertainment for everybody in the form of a water show at the fountain outside the gate every evening at 9pm. *Daily 9am–9pm | basic package (90 mins) incl. two massages 60 euros | on the coastal road to the west of the roundabout | tel. 22 42 06 72 70 72 | artemishamam.com*

Flamingos are seasonal visitors to the Alikés Salt Lake

MARMÁRI

(G2) **Before the tourists arrived, Marmári (pop. 460) was the landing place for the fishermen of Pýli.**

These days, Marmári has turned into a cluster of smaller and larger hotels, which are all built a good distance from each other. They all enjoy the use of the village's miles of wide sandy beach. In the centre and in front of the larger hotels, the beach has sun loungers and parasols; other sections lie as empty as they always did in front of a belt of low dunes. Between June and November you're bound to see grazing cows. They are allowed to feed on what's left on the fields after the grain harvest, and like taking the odd trip to the beach.

EATING & DRINKING

ROSE

This rather simple Greek taverna is a favourite among families. Kids love the pizza, the pasta and the small playground. *Daily | main road, approx. 400m from the beach | €*

SMILEY'S

This roadside grill bar serves no-frills, yet tasty and extremely affordable food. Take in the sea views while you enjoy a *moussaká*, Greek salad or mixed grill. *Daily | where the main road meets the beach | €*

SPORT & ACTIVITIES

CHRÍSTOS GO KARTS

Many holiday islands boast go-kart tracks, but Chrístos Go Karts at Marmári goes one step further and thinks of the little ones too. While the adults hare through the bends on their powerful karts, three- to nine-year olds can go round and round on a separate track on  electric karts. There is yet another track for toddlers. *Daily 9.30am–11pm | large karts approx. 25 euros/20 mins, electric karts from approx. 6 euros/10 mins | on the road between Marmári and Tigáki*

ERIKA'S HORSE FARM

Like most riding stables on the island, Erika also offers hacks on the beach and across the fields. However, what is special are her popular café and the child-friendly atmosphere, including lessons and rides for children. Her farm is home to the little Skýros horses, an endangered species from an island in the archipelago of the Northern Sporades. Erika has goats and sheep to pet, chickens and ducks to feed and a playground. She also offers therapeutic horse riding. The transfer to the farm from all hotels between the town and Mastichári is free of charge. *Odós Possidónos | tel. 69 45 93 51 37 | erikashorsefarm.gr*

WATERSPORTS

See the Sport & Activities chapter (p. 32).

BEACHES

Marmári Beach stretches from the salt lake in the east to Mastichári in the west. Between the beaches in front of the hotels, such as *Carávia Beach*, there is still plenty of sand free from loungers and parasols.

NIGHTLIFE

Marmári is not exactly Club Central. The few holidaymakers who leave the no-pay area of their all-inclusive resort after their evening buffet prefer to sit in airy garden bars listening to good music, and maybe enjoy the occasional late-night boogie.

MASTICHÁRI

(□ E3) **Of the three holiday spots on the northern coast, Mastichári has best managed to hold on to some of its village character.**

Mastichári's minuscule centre has Mediterreanean flair; even in winter the village retains some of its charm. The small harbour is a hub of activity all year round because ferries, mainly used by locals, depart from here several times a day to Kálimnos. There is a wide stretch of sandy beach directly in front of the hotels and small self-catering apartments for those wanting a more individual holiday experience. There is more going on here in the evenings than in Tigáki and Marmári where all-inclusive hotels have ruined the nightlife.

SIGHTSEEING

ÁGIOS IOÁNNIS BASILICA

A few walls, one or two columns and mosaic ruins scattered among the grass are all that is left of this early Christian chapel next to the sea. Only the cross-shaped font set into the floor sparks the imagination of what it was like 1,500 years ago when crowds of people would have been baptized by full immersion in this font. *Freely accessible | signposted on the road to the east of the Euro Village Achillea Hotel | can also be reached on foot along the beach from the village centre | ○ 10 mins*

Just a few more metres, and you have made it to long Marmári Beach!

ÁGIOS GEÓRGIOS LOÍZOS CHURCH

A romantic spot and the perfect photo opportunity: perched on a lonely outcrop on the edge of the barren, hilly landscape is this medieval, blue-and-white painted chapel, resembling a Greek flag made of stone. On closer inspection, you will notice that the chapel was built on the ruins of an early Christian basilica, the original walls of which can still be seen. The door is usually kept open; St George is pleased to receive visitors whatever time of day. Why not enter and light a candle? *Coming from Kos Town, the church is on the right-hand side of the road, just over 1.5km after leaving the main road in the direction of Mastichári |* ⏱ *10 mins*

SCULPTURE PARK 🐖

In the grounds of one of the island's foremost hotels, the Bavarian sculptor Peter R. Müller was allowed to recreate the world of ancient gods and myths from iron and scrap metal. Here, Zeus is throwing neon-coloured lightning, Prometheus is bringing fire to humans, and Poseidon is guiding his rusty steeds. *Sculpture park freely accessible | Neptune Resort | between Mastichári and Marmári |* ⏱ *20–30 mins*

EATING & DRINKING

KALÍ KARDIÁ

At its inauguration in 1955, the "Good Heart" was the only restaurant for miles around. The old hospitality is still there, while the range of food has been adapted to the needs of holiday-makers. A whole dentex fish with boiled potatoes and fresh vegetables is charged at a fixed price, rather than by weight, as is often the case elsewhere. Early birds like to come here for a morning coffee; it's the only place open at 7am. *Daily | at the harbour across from the bus stop | €*

PERIKLÍS

Periklís, the host of this restaurant, rejects gastronomic globalisation. You order fish, you get fish – and no fries with that. Side dishes are ordered separately. Calamari from the freezer is cheap; or it's a bit more expensive fresh from the Aegean Sea. If they are on the menu, make sure you go for the tiny prawns from the island of Sými, which are a speciality. **INSIDER TIP** **Trust Periklís!** Regular guests let the host choose their meal and only tell him how much they are willing to spend. *Daily | at the harbour | €€€*

TAM TAM ⭐

This garden taverna is located on a dune right on broad sandy 🏖 *Tam Tam Beach*; cows graze on the pastures beyond. Children find plenty of space for games, adults up for a chat can sit at the inviting bar, and shopaholics can browse breezy beachwear and costume jewellery in the shop reminiscent of the hippie era. The choice of dishes ranges from pizza to fresh fish. *Daily | 3km east of Mastichári | €€*

Light a candle to St George at the Ágios Geórgios Loízos chapel

TRADITIONAL GREEK HOUSE

Natural stone walls and a room furnished like a traditional farmhouse with a stone oven still used for producing home-made bread are the hallmarks of this restaurant on the western beach of Mastichári. The 👶 children's playground in the direction of the beach makes it easy to distinguish this establishment from its competitors which bear almost identical names. Host Sávvas and his wife Ioánna take great care to only source chicken, meat, cheese and many other ingredients from their relations, enabling them to guarantee freshness and quality. Portions are large and on the rustic and hearty side, with lots of high-quality olive oil used in the cooking. If you don't like it quite so oily, just say *"me polí lígo ládi, parakaló"* (with very little oil)! Daily | access from the beach west of the harbour, or from the one-way road leading out of the village (look for a small signpost) | €

INSIDER TIP
Oil as requested

SHOPPING

PIA & IRA

While the two women owners don't produce any of the jewellery and souvenirs for sale, they have excellent taste. Both are also cat lovers and animal welfare activists, always happy to receive pet food donations for their charges. *On the main pedestrian street*

SPORT & ACTIVITIES

Car ferries connect Mastichári with Póthia, the capital of the neighbouring island of Kálimnos, at least three times a day. There is also a small and quick passenger ferry which runs up to six times daily and whose timetable is aligned with the arrival and departure of scheduled flights from and to Athens. *For timetables visit anem ferries.gr and portofkalymnos.com.*

BEACHES

Along the miles of sandy beach starting immediately west and east of Mastichári harbour, you can find sections with shade-giving tamarisks. A little east from the harbour there is a short section of beach in front of some low cliffs. Between Mastichári and Marmári dunes run along the broad band of sand; many sections of the beach here are free of sunshades and sun loungers.

Two uncrowded beaches are situated outside Mastichári between the Euro Village Hotel and the island's power plant: *Dolphin Bay Beach* with a garden taverna that serves highly acclaimed mojitos and *Prótokaravas Beach* with the *Lovely Beach* taverna whose rural landlords are very friendly.

WELLNESS

In the old village centre, physiotherapist Kóstas Fessarás offers professional massage in a matter-of-fact ambience *(village centre, on the lane that runs parallel to the beach | tel. 69 77 78 47 90 | mastichari-massage.gr).* He also does home visits to your hotel room or apartment.

NIGHTLIFE

NUMBER ONE BAR

A sea of flowers and grapevines cover the terrace, under which you can enjoy cocktails and a cool beer on tap, making this bar the "number one" hotspot in the village. The owner plays vinyl records – and if enough guests are in party mood, the dance floor inside will fill up. *Daily from around 6pm | between the one-way street leading out of the village and the western beach*

AROUND MASTICHÁRI

1 ANCIENT HOUSE – HIPPOCRATES GARDEN

7km / 15 mins from Mastichári by car
When Julie Zafeirátou serves you a free herbal tea under the shady trees in her garden, you are sitting in front of a follower of the father of medicine, Hippocrates. She is a true believer in his therapeutic approach based on the healing power of nature. In this little-known place located in the middle of nowhere, she grows herbs and plants in the same wild conditions they would have enjoyed in ancient times, without beds and borders and 100% organic. To transport her guests

back to Hippocrates's time, she has reconstructed a house and furnished it as it would have been in ancient times – including a toilet with a flushing system. *Daily 9am–9pm | admission 5 euros | on a dirt road between the airport and the north coast, signposted | hippocratesgarden.gr | 40 mins–1 hr | D4*

ZÍA

(H3) **Can you make a living from the sunset? In Zía, you can! Although Kos offers many great places to watch the sun go down, every tourist wants to see the sun plunge into the Aegean from this particular spot.**

In high season, it is best to book a table in advance. The tavernas have aligned their terraces in the direction of the sunset and many locals who do not own a restaurant have opened a souvenir shop instead. The best place to park is uphill near the Natural Park. Walk down the main street to the small *platía* and then walk to the highest part of the village. You'll pass an old water mill and reach the village chapel with the prettiest sunset terraces. Once you've watched the spectacle, stroll down the non-touristy lane back to your car.

SIGHTSEEING

MISSIS TIS THEOTÓKOU CHURCH
Have you ever seen an archangel bearing the fuse box for the church lighting

Number One Bar: cold beer and vinyl records

on his chest? The electrician thought this would be the most practical place for it in the village church that is dedicated to the Virgin Mary. You'll find the unique masterpiece on the left-hand wall. The entire interior, including the archangel and the other frescoes, was painted between 1992 and 1995.

Two of the frescoes portray stories from the Bible unknown to most people. On one, Jesus breaks down the gates of Hell to lead the dead to eternal life, the first of whom were Adam and Eve. On the opposite wall on the right, you can see the Dormition – literally the falling asleep – of the Virgin Mary. Jesus and the Apostles are standing at the deathbed of the Virgin Mary, and Jesus has already taken her

soul, represented as a swaddled child, into his hands, to take it to heaven. *Open all day | ⏱ 10–20 mins*

EATING & DRINKING

NERÓMILOS ⭐

Guess how many miles lie between you and London, New York or Moscow? You'll find the answer on the many signposts on the colourful terrace of this lively taverna. And if your hometown is missing, simply bring a sign the next time you visit; the landlord will fix it for you. Otherwise, sit back and relax in the shade, sip a glass of home-made lemonade and

INSIDER TIP
Far from home?

Bright colours of the Aegean on a typical terrace in Zía

try a piece of home-made cake. *Daily | between platía and village church | €*

OROMÉDON ⚑

Ready, steady – sunset! Everybody wants to see this spectacle in Zía and the local restaurants specialise in the event. This well-kept taverna, run by a local family, has great views from the terrace overgrown with bougainvillea. They also serve vegan and gluten-free dishes. You can book online. *Daily | at the bottom entrance to the village | tel. 22 42 06 99 83 | oromedon.com | €€*

SUNSET BALCONY ☂

Stérgos and his wife Chrissoúla were the first to come up with the idea of marketing this natural spectacle in Zía. And they are still serving guests with the same enthusiasm and the same classic dishes on the menu: delicious *souvláki*, grilled courgettes and aubergines and *revithókeftédes*, a type of potato pancake made from chickpea flour. And only Greek music is played to serenade the sunset. *Daily | just below the village church | €*

SHOPPING

If you're after authentic souvenirs, this is not the place to come to, as nothing is produced in Zía any more. All the wares on offer come from elsewhere in Greece, if not from further afield.

SPORT & ACTIVITIES

NATURAL PARK ZÍA 🐾

On the eastern edge of Zía, along the slope above the road to the Asklípion, is a small forest park with pretty trails, a playground, a few watercourses and some animals such as peacocks, ducks, goats and rabbits. Great for parents and children alike, because the ticket allows you to enter the park repeatedly during the day, so that a visit makes a welcome reward! *Daily 10am–30 mins after sunset | admission 4 euros, children (aged 3–12) 2 euros | kosnaturalpark.gr*

AROUND ZÍA

🔢 MOUNT DÍKEOS

8km return hike, approx. 500m height difference / 4-5 hrs from Zía on foot

Zía is the base for climbing Díkeos (843m), the island's highest mountain. Depending on fitness levels, hikers need between four and five hours to go up and back down. The footpath starts at the small, cobbled square in the upper part of the village, where you'll usually see some cars parked. From here, steps leading uphill join a track, from which more steps lead to an unpaved road that you follow uphill to the right. At the next fork in the road, marked by a bell hanging in a tree belonging to the *Isódia tis Theotókou* chapel, keep right. After a few minutes, a steep track forks off uphill to the left, marked by a signpost with a white cross on a red background. From here, the remaining path to the summit is marked by red dots. Just before you reach the highest point on Díkeos, the

Metamórfosis tou Christoú chapel announces the presence of a monastery that has been here since the late 11th century.

Minimum requirements for the hike are shoes with good grip, something to cover your head, and water. If you can, start the tour in the early morning so that you are already descending when the midday heat hits. ⌘ *H–J3*

3 LAGOÚDI ★

3km / 6 mins from Zía by car
Are you dreaming of a beautiful, tranquil village with no other tourists but which is still appealing and hospitable? Then look no further – Lagoúdi is for you. This hamlet with only 30 inhabitants is located just 500m off the main road from Zía to Kos Town, yet it has been spared most of the onslaught of mass tourism. Cockerels are free to roam on the village street, and in the *kafeníon* time seems to have stood still. The centre of the village is marked by the slightly elevated *Panagía Theotókou Genesíou* church (*daily 11am–6pm* | ⏱ *10–20 mins*) dedicated to the birth of the Virgin Mary. The extremely friendly village priest Kyriákos lived for a while in Germany, which explains why he speaks a little German. If he's not around, his very talkative sacristan, Dobrinka from Bulgaria, will help. She also sells her soft toys and baskets made of newspaper in the churchyard. Painted between 1985 and 1997, the church's frescoes tell a story. Unusually, you are allowed to take photos of them.

Next to the lane heading up to the church, a track leads down and after only 20m passes the fascinating *I Oréa Elláda (Beautiful Greece)* estate (*café and shops Fri–Wed 10am–10pm* | *tel. 22 42 06 90 04, mobile 69 73 49 20 31* | *€€*). A Flemish woman, Christina Zentéli-Colman, who has lived here for decades, has turned the place into a paradise for lovers of antiques, painting and jewellery, as well as good food and drink. Four holiday apartments have that truly rural holiday feeling. ⌘ *H3*

PÝLI

(⌘ *G3*) **A village virtually devoid of tourists? Yes, this really can be found on Kos. With 2,600 inhabitants, Pýli is the largest inland village on the island – and none of the inhabitants officially let guest rooms.**

You can still watch local life pass by on the village square. At the main crossroads in the lower part of the village, young men from a nearby refugee camp wait for pickups to take them to the fields for casual work. They are lucky if they get paid 2 euros an hour for their hard work.

SIGHTSEEING

VILLAGE FOUNTAIN
When was the last time you drank fresh water straight from the lion's mouth? Water has been pouring from this fountain built on stone blocks in

Pýli since 1592. *Freely accessible | 150m west of the village square |* ⏱ *5 mins*

TOMB OF HARMYLOS ★

You may find yourself falling in love with this magical and mystical site in the centre of the village. Ancient Koans believed this vaulted tomb chamber with six niches on its two longer sides to be the mausoleum of Harmylos, the mythical founding father of Koa's first ruling dynasty. In medieval times the back wall of the colonnade above was used as a small chapel. On the west side, two beautiful ancient blocks with a relief frieze were inserted into the chapel wall. A nearly hidden signpost on a sharp right-hand bend on the tarmacked road leading to Kardámena points the way to the tomb. *Freely accessible during the day | approx. 5 mins from the village square |* ⏱ *10 mins*

EVANGELISMÓS CHURCH

Like many of the churches and chapels throughout Greece, this chapel is painted in stages, bit by bit, just as soon as the church receives a donation. Since 1987, the parishioners have been trying to represent heaven on earth in this tiny chapel. *Open during the day | on the village square |* ⏱ *5–10 mins*

EATING & DRINKING

PALIÁ PIGÍ (OLD WATERSPRING) ★

In this small taverna by the village fountain, Geórgios and Evangelía spoil

Lagoúdi church in the evening light: the views from Zía are truly fabulous!

their guests below a shady *ficus benjamina* tree with delicious fried aubergine and courgette slices, small *soúvlaki* skewers and *sousoukákia* sausages from the charcoal grill. *Daily | €*

AROUND PÝLI

⁴ OLD PÝLI (PALÉA PÝLI) ★

3.5km / 10 mins from Pýli by car
Two summits in one day: on top of the first are the *ruins of a castle*. The path leads you through an abandoned village which was deserted in 1839 after a cholera epidemic; only four medieval churches are left standing. You are treated to wonderful views of the 11th-century castle from the neighbouring summit where Geórgios and Michális have turned the house in which they were born into a cosy *café (daily | €)*. Salads and small snacks are always available and sometimes they light the barbecue for guests. *Accessible from Pýli via Amianoú. The tarmacked road stops beneath the castle and is the starting point for the paths up to the castle and café; you can only continue up the road by jeep or mountain bike |* ⏱ *1–2 hrs, walking time (without stops) approx. 1 hr |* 🗺 *H3*

INSIDER TIP
Great views

Delicacies served at the Paliá Pigí taverna: it doesn't get more Greek

ANTIMÁCHIA

(□ E4) **Antimáchia, situated on a high plain in the centre of the island, is the second-largest inland village on Kos (pop. 2,200).**

In the 1920s, the sailcloth-covered blades of over 100 windmills were still turning in Antimáchia. Today, there is not a lot to see here and you'll probably want to move on after 50 minutes at the most.

SIGHTSEEING

TRADITIONAL HOUSE ★ ☂

Antimáchia's cultural association has converted an old farmhouse diagonally opposite the windmill into a kind of folklore museum. Here you can see the way a 14-strong Antimáchia family would have lived up until the 1950s. One of the three rooms in the main house contained the stables, while an extension holds a loom and an oven. A stone basin in the front courtyard served to store the water which did not flow from pipes but had to be fetched from the village well. *Mon–Sat 9am–5pm, Sun 11am–3pm | admission 2 euros | ⏱ 10–15 mins*

WINDMILL ☂

Since 2014, the canvas blades of the windmill have been turning once again. You can now tour the mill, take a selfie and have a break in the adjacent café, enjoying their cakes and pastries made from the flour which is milled here. *Daily 9am–5.30pm | admission 3 euros | ⏱ 10–15 mins*

AROUND ANTIMÁCHIA

🟧 ANTIMÁCHIA CASTLE (KÁSTRO)

4km / 10 mins from Antimáchia by car

The road leading to Antimáchia Castle crosses a rugged high plain, with the long line of crenellations on the island's most impressive fortification looming against the sky from afar. The road ends in front of the northern gate of the fortification, which also served as a place of refuge. It was started by the Venetians in the 13th century and was completed by the Knights of St John in the 14th century. Once you've walked through the outer gate, you are standing in front of a second gate, where the coat of arms of the Grand Master of the Order, Pierre d'Aubusson, and the year 1494 can still be made out. Practically nothing remains of the buildings inside the fortifications other than a few cisterns and two small churches that stand amidst the rampant vegetation.

Finally, from the southern edge of the castle there are some nice views over the extensive fertile coastal plain of Kardámena and across to the volcanic neighbouring island of Níssiros. Access is signposted from the main road east of Antimáchia. *Freely accessible at all times | ⏱ 45 mins–1 hr | □ F4*

KARDÁMENA

(🗺 *G5*) **The reputation of Kardámena, the only true village on the southern coast, is gradually improving.**

After years of disrepute dating back to the beginning of the 2000s, when British hooligans behaved so shockingly that some Koan taxi drivers refused to take them in their cabs, the resort has cleaned up its image.

Some of the old clubs and pubs still exist, although refurbished, and the large hotels along the beaches are now geared towards families. Kardámena is more family-friendly, but its nightlife is still livelier than that of Tigáki, Marmári and Mastichári together. The holiday hotels are all situated on the relatively narrow strip of beach on both sides of the resort, up to 7km away from the centre. In summer, a bus commutes between Kardámena and Kos Town. The centre consists of three parallel streets and the long harbour promenade, lined with cafés, bars and shops. Rising up out of the Aegean in front of the harbour is the volcanic outcrop of Níssiros, and boats ferry passengers over to this small island every day. If you're based elsewhere on the island, Kardámena is only worth visiting for an hour for a coffee on the harbour promenade.

EATING & DRINKING

AVLÍ
The inner courtyard is an Aegean idyll, serving a variety of small dishes and vegetarian delicacies. The wine cellar stores about 70 different wines from all over the world. *Daily from 5pm | Platía | avlirestaurant.gr | €€€*

GARDEN BAR
If you're looking for a snack, a sweet treat or a freshly made salad, then the Garden Bar, run by Jack and Dimítri, is the right place. Under the sweet-smelling jasmine, relax on the colourful cushioned seats in front of one of the oldest preserved houses in the village, built in 1943. And if you're not driving home, try the house speciality – organically grown wines. *Daily | first parallel street to the harbour promenade close to the platía | €*

INSIDER TIP
Organic wine from Kos

LOVEMADE BAKERY
If you don't have breakfast in your hotel, this bakery with its extensive menu should be your first choice. And it is a good place to come at any time of day if you like vegetarian and vegan food. *Daily | Odós Thymáton 9 | €*

O DÁSKALOS
The proprietor decides which appetisers to serve with the ouzo, whereas customers are free to choose which desserts, *gliká tou koutoulioú*, they would like: quinces, cherry tomatoes or bergamots soaked in syrup. If you're feeling brave, sample the *masticha*, a cream made from sugar and the resin from the mastic tree. *Open at the discretion of the owner |*

INSIDER TIP
Drink tree resin

KARDÁMENA

Pýli - Kardámena

Sofokleous

I. Kanári

28is Oktovríou

Sokratous

Pýli - Kardámena

Garden Bar

Pélagos

O Dáskalos

Lovemade Bakery

Downtown

Avlí

Deligusto

Kardámaina - Antimáchia
Kardámena - Antimáchia

Alasarnas

Akti Miaouli

Lizy's

Skála

A i g a i o n   P e l a g o s

Liménískos Kardamaína

200 m
218 yd

between the 1st & 2nd streets parallel to the harbour promenade | €

PÉLAGOS

Despite the restaurant's size and its extensive menu, the dishes created by hosts Jánnis and Dimítris are excellent! They will advise you on which dishes to choose, and you will get great value for your money. *Daily | eastern shoreline promenade | €€*

SHOPPING

DELIGUSTO

If you like good wine, visit this wine store with its unusually decorated interior and a huge range of excellent Greek wines and spirits. They also have eccentric crisps. *Odós 28is Oktovríou*

LIZY'S

Apart from all kinds of textiles, this shop has an interesting selection of Greek designer jewellery for all budgets. *Odós 25is Martíou*

SPORT & ACTIVITIES

AQUATICA WATER PARK

Children will love this water park with its numerous slides of all sizes. Although it belongs to a hotel, it is also open to non-residents. The park is not too big and has a cafeteria on site. *May–Oct daily 10.30am–5.30pm | admission 16 euros, children from 1.20m in height 12 euros, smaller children go free | 3km east of the Porto Bello Beach and Royal hotels | aquatica.gr | scheduled local buses*

Kardámena's harbour promenade is a great place to enjoy a cup of coffee

ORGANISED EXCURSIONS

Excursion coaches to Paradise Beach *(return trip 7 euros)*; passenger ferries to the neighbouring island of Níssiros *(Mon–Sat approx. 2pm)*, excursion boats *(daily approx. 9am)*.

SPORT

The area offers water sports and riding *(see the Sport & activities chapter, p. 32)*.

WELLNESS

PRANA YOGA SHALA

Christina Gougousális offers a range of yoga sessions and meditation for both local people and holidaymakers all year round. Please book in advance on FB or by phone. *Odós Sokratoús/ corner of Odós Dimokratías | tel. 69 85 76 13 56 | from 12 euros/hr*

BEACHES

Immediately east of the harbour is a tiny and always-busy sandy beach. Otherwise, people bathe on a relatively narrow, 7km-long sand-and-pebble beach that stretches away on either side of the town. It is covered in 60-year-old bunkers which were intended to protect Kos from an invasion by NATO ally Turkey, but now these fortifications are dilapidated and blown over by the sand. There is a local bus offering an approx. hourly

service from the main square by the harbour to the Norída Beach hotel in the east and the Aegean Village hotel in the west.

NIGHTLIFE

DOWNTOWN
This relatively small club plays international music but it is nevertheless frequented by many Greek people.

SKÁLA
The Chrysopoulos family runs the best-known cocktail bar on Kos in a building that is more than 110 years old. Nowhere else can you choose from a greater selection of gins or enjoy a better cheesecake. From the roof terrace you have great views across palm trees to the sea and the opposite island of Níssiros. *Directly east of the harbour*

WHERE TO STAY IN THE CENTRE

TENTS AMONG TREES
You won't find a more original and eco-friendly place to stay on the island than the *Sails on Kos* tent hotel *(south-west of Marmári centre | tel. 69 72 07 00 53 | sailsonkos. com)*. A verdant plot of land by the sea houses 16 tent villas and ten bell tents. The resort includes a pool and vegetable patch, the restaurant focuses on local produce and guests can hire bicycles and e-bikes as well as drones for taking their own aerial shots.

NEPTUNE RESORT
Do you like large, spacious and luxurious beach resorts which offer a wide range of activities? Then you'll feel right at home in this first-class complex *(Mastichári–Marmári road | tel. 22 42 04 14 80 | neptune.gr | €€€)*, right next to the beach with four pools, a spa, water sport activities, mountain bikes, tennis, squash and childcare facilities. The resort is committed to sustainability and you can read about its environmental, employee and human rights policies in the hotel's brochures.

THE WEST

A single village is nestled among the wild and sparse vegetation that covers the west of the island. Most of the soil is barren, with only juniper thriving in many places. In the spring, when herbs and rock-roses are in bloom, the whole area is enveloped in the fragrance of thyme and oregano.

Fourteen kilometres to the west of the airport, the road that runs along the backbone of the island merges into a large coastal plain known as the Kámbos plain. A few small B&Bs and tavernas are scattered among

There's a great bathing spot by the remains of the early Christian basilica of Ágios Stéfanos

deserted fields. Only minutes away, yet hidden from the road, are a multitude of superb sandy beaches – the wealth of this area.

The winding road takes you uphill to the village of Kéfalos, where another world begins: the idyllically rural Kéfalos peninsula, where time appears to have stood still. Sheep and goats roam the green hillside, swarms of bees collect thyme pollen, while a handful of chapels and a deserted monastery dot the landscape. Apart from two tavernas, these coastal roads are devoid of buildings.

THE WEST

7 Limniónas

5km, 10 mins

Milies

Ágios Stéfanos Basilica ★ ⚲

Κέφαλος

Kéfalos
p. 90

Kolpos
Kefalou

Καμάρι
Kamari

3 Panagía
i Palianí Church

4 Ancient Theatre of Palatia

7km, 15 mins

6 Panagía Stylóti
Church

Theológos Beach

5 Ágios Ioánnis Pródromos Monastery ★

10km, 15 mins

Magic Beach

Polémi Beach ★

Paradise Beach ★

1 Camel Beach

2

MARCO POLO HIGHLIGHTS

★ **ÁGIOS STÉFANOS BASILICA**
No need to cover up here: a bikini is
standard attire in the ruins of the former
St Stephen's church, right on the beach
➤ p. 90

★ **PARADISE BEACH**
Everyone is in search of paradise, which
is why this beach is often crowded
➤ p. 92

★ **ÁGIOS IOÁNNIS PRÓDROMOS
MONASTERY**
While away the hours in the small café
of this deserted monastery ➤ p. 94

★ **POLÉMI BEACH**
Skinny dipping is a popular pastime at
this beach ➤ p. 96

A i g a i o n

P e l a g o s

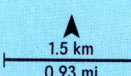

1.5 km
0.93 mi

KÉFALOS

(⊞ B6) **A village, lots of unspoilt nature and endless beaches: the island's west is predominantly for bathing, and possibly hiking. Kéfalos was the first ancient settlement on the island. It was abandoned only when an earthquake destroyed the town in 412 BCE and the inhabitants left to found Kos Town.**

There are very few traces of antiquity left in Kéfalos itself. Today, the village appears sleepy and insignificant – it's worth a coffee break, but that's about all.

SIGHTSEEING

ÁGIOS STÉFANOS BASILICA ★

Sunbathing inside a church? That's sort of possible on the beach opposite the small island of Kastrí, where you can spread out your towel between columns and 1,500-year-old walls then jump into the sea just ten paces away. Italian archaeologists restored a few of the columns and placed them upright – most, however, have since fallen over again.

INSIDER TIP
Sunbathe at church

The layout of the three-naved basilica can still be made out. Against the northern wall stood a second, smaller church with a cruciform baptismal font on the floor that is very well preserved. Floor mosaics found here were covered up again with gravel. *Accessible at all times | on the beach immediately west of the Ikos Resort; access from the main road via the narrow road beginning immediately to the right of the resort's barrier | ⏱ visit to the basilica 10 mins*

RUINED CASTLE

As with many other places, the medieval village of Kéfalos was once protected by a castle, of which now only a few walls remain. The view, which stretches across the coastal plain below, remains intact. *Freely accessible | on reaching the mountain village, immediately turn off to the right | ⏱ 5 mins*

KASTRÍ ISLAND

The tiny rocky island, just offshore the Ágios Stéfanos basilica is uninhabited. All there is to see is a small and usually locked church dedicated to St Nicholas. It is possible to reach the islet by wading and sometimes swimming a route between buoys, which are there to stop motorboats and windsurfers from passing.

INSIDER TIP
Not suitable for non-swimmers

ISÓDIA TIS PANAGÍAS CHURCH

The main church in Kéfalos is dedicated to the Entry into The Temple of the Most Holy Mother of God. It was funded in 1873 by a high-ranking official from Egypt, which like Kos was once part of the Ottoman Empire. Inside, the church is completely covered in murals in the traditional Byzantine style. *Usually open in the morning | ⏱ 5–10 mins*

EATING & DRINKING

FYTÓRIO 🐷

The small family-owned taverna right on the road from the airport to Kéfalos is the cheapest place to eat in this part of the island. Servings are generous, prices are reasonable and the landlord's family looks after their guests beautifully. *Daily | €*

KATERINA

One beach, one taverna – what more could you wish for? Hopefully nothing, because that's all there is at the western end of Ágios Stéfanos Beach. The taverna uses local ingredients with freshly caught fish, eggs laid by their own chickens, lettuce and vegetables from the island's farmers and the whole family helps out with the service. *Daily | €*

MYLOTOPI

A few years ago, the Voudoúris family restored some rural buildings high above the Bay of Kéfalos and developed them into a free museum with a stylish café, bar and restaurant. The visual centrepiece is a fully operational historic windmill. The functioning stone oven was built using volcanic rock from Níssiros, and you can often see a donkey in the threshing place. The wine cellar is now in a 20m-long tunnel from the time of the Italian occupation. In one of the old farmhouses, the museum where you can learn how people lived on the island 150 years ago. The other farmhouse was constructed from natural stone and wood from the holy mountain of Áthos in northern Greece and now features the restaurant which serves many superb, traditional Greek dishes. *Daily 9am–1am | on the ring road past the castle | tel. 22 42 07 30 00 | mylotopi.com | €€*

It is possible to swim across to Kastrí Island

SHOPPING

Neither Kéfalos nor Kámbos have large supermarkets or souvenir shops, but you can get groceries and everyday items from several small shops in either place. Since you can see sheep roaming freely everywhere, you really must try the local Kéfalos sheep's milk cheese.

INSIDER TIP
Baa!

BEACHES

KÁMBOS BEACH

In the western part of Kámbos, the beach is only a few metres wide, running immediately below the road. From the jetty in *Skála* onwards the beach becomes wider again, and prettier, too, with the most beautiful part between the Ágios Stéfanos Basilica and the Katerína taverna.

WELLNESS

If you want to combine holiday and wellness treatments in this part of the island, you need to stay at the *Blue Lagoon Village* hotel *(bluelagoonvillage.gr)*, otherwise you will have to resort to mobile massage therapists at Kámbos Beach or on Paradise Beach.

NIGHTLIFE

B 52

Kéfalos goes to bed early. The only sign of nightlife is this popular hangout on the promenade which serves good cocktails and plays mainly hip-hop, soul and R&B. *On the coastal road between Skála and Kamári next to the small Hotel Sydney*

CARAMELA CLUB

The doors of the only club for miles, in Kámbos, around usually open at the weekends all year round. The music is geared toward the locals, playing both Greek rock and traditional sounds. Check out the posters! *Kámbos | on the main road to the airport | FB: caramela club kefalos-kos*

BUSES & FERRIES

Bus connection with Kos Town *(Mon–Sat 4 to 6 times a day, Sun 3 times daily)*. If you want to go to Kardámena, change in Antimáchia.

In the summer season, a ferry runs to the beautiful neighbouring island of Níssiros *(up to five times a week)*.

AROUND KÉFALOS

1 CAMEL BEACH 🌴

5km / 15 mins from Kéfalos by moped

A steep unmade road leads down to this small remote bay between the 3km-long beaches at Kéfalos. The beach here is only about 100m long; climbing over rocks will lead you to other tiny sandy spots, where nudist bathing is an option. Of all the beaches around Kéfalos this is the most attractive for snorkellers. Two simple tavernas compete for guests. The access is signposted from the main road, 600m away. *C6*

2 PARADISE BEACH ⭐ 🌴

6km / 15 mins from Kéfalos by bus

If you think solitary, deserted beaches are overrated, then this beach may be the strip of paradise you've been searching for your whole life. Row upon row of parasols and sun loungers line up along the sand, and you'll never feel alone.

Kéfalos beaches have the right winds for windsurfers, both beginners and professionals

A good watersports centre offers everything from parasailing, jet- and waterskiing to crazy sofa, flyfish and pedalos. Sand covers the slopes rising steeply behind the beach, making them look like high dunes. The eastern part of Paradise Beach is also known as *Bubble Beach*. It owes its name to a fascinating natural phenomenon which can be enjoyed by snorkellers and divers: in the sunshine, the many bubbles rising up from the bottom of the sea sparkle like diamonds. For a particularly romantic experience, try a full-moon swim, when a dancing veil of luminous bubbles surrounds the swimmers.

INSIDER TIP
Bubble magic

The busy beach bar, with its palm roof, appears to have been transported here from the South Pacific. From the café-restaurant further up the hillside (*daily* | *€€€*) you have magnificent views of the 10km-long beach to the Robinson Club at the end. There are plenty of car parking spaces available and the bus operating between Kéfalos and Kos Town makes a detour up here. *C6*

❸ PANAGÍA I PALATIANÍ CHURCH

1km / 20 mins from Kéfalos on foot
The small chapel, built in 1988 and given whitewashed walls and a blue vaulted ceiling, can be seen for miles, without having much of architectural interest. However, only 15m away, a ruined chapel dedicated to the Virgin Mary was erected using carefully worked blocks of an ancient temple which used to stand here. *The modern chapel is always locked, the ruins are freely accessible | 200m off the tarmacked road leading to the Ágios*

Sun, sea and cliffs: dreamlike bays near Kéfalos

Ioánnis Pródromos monastery | ⏱ 5–10 mins | 🗺 B7

4 ANCIENT THEATRE OF PALATIA

1.5km / 30 mins from Kéfalos on foot
The remains of the theatre of the ancient town of Palatia lie amidst a fragrant pine forest on the edge of a deep gorge. The only thing to see now are the remnants of two rows of seats and a few fragments of the stage building from the second century BCE (Hellenistic era). Ten metres left of the exit you can spot very sparse remains of an ancient Demeter sanctuary. *The path to the theatre complex is to the left of the tarmacked road leading to the Ágios Ioánnis Pródromos*

monastery; after about 30m, there's a gate in the wire fence (always open) | ⏱ 10 mins | 🗺 B6

5 ÁGIOS IOÁNNIS PRÓDROMOS MONASTERY ⭐

7km / 15 mins from Kéfalos by car
The sound of goats' bells can be heard in the distance and the smell of thyme tickles your nose: sitting under the shade of the mulberry trees taking in the panoramic views of the sea and the passing ships below, you become all too aware of the significance of this holy place. The taverna's landlady Katarina serves salads, tzatziki, chickpea patties, toasted sandwiches and drinks – what more could you want?

to have been built for one single event in the year: the feast days on 14/15 August. Inside, the little church is fairly devoid of decoration, but the stone tables and benches around it can accommodate over 1,000 participants. Every year, people come in large numbers to enjoy the typical feast of chickpea soup and grilled lamb or kid goat, washed down with wine or ouzo. *1,300m off the access road to Ágios Theológos, signposted in Greek only | church key hanging above the door |* □ *B7*

7 LIMNIÓNAS

5km / 10 mins from Kéfalos by car

The essence of Kos is brought together in the most north-westerly point of the island. What more could you need than two small beaches, a fishing harbour and one taverna *(€€€)*, which prepares and serves the freshly caught fish? Other than that, you won't find anything and the road ends at the water's edge. If you can see tourist coaches parked outside the taverna, brave yourself for a long wait to be served. □ *B5*

INSIDER TIP
Better avoid the coaches

SOUTH COAST BEACHES

8–13km / 20–40 mins from Kéfalos by moped

Beaches with virtually no end in sight: the wide strip of sandy beach along the south coast stretches from *Paradise Beach* all the way down to *Golden Beach* and beyond. The only blot on the horizon is the massive hotel complex hidden in a valley behind Golden Beach; other than that,

The freshly painted monastery church is worth a peep inside and maybe you can light a candle. There are only ruins now where the cells once stood, and the old bell in the tree is only rung on two days in August – the 28th and 29th – when hundreds of pilgrims come here to pray, eat, drink and dance together. *Freely accessible | 2.5km past the fork to Panagía Ziniótissa, a small, tarmacked road branches off to the monastery, only 200m away |* ○ *15–45 mins |* □ *B7*

6 PANAGÍA STYLÓTI CHURCH ⚑

4km / 10 mins from Kéfalos by car

Dedicated to the Virgin Mary, this church in a lonely landscape appears

Beautiful and remote: Theológos Beach on the west coast

no building permits have been granted in this region.

Only a handful of tavernas are scattered on the hillside slightly above the beach at a suitable distance apart. Small dirt tracks branch off from the island's main thoroughfare and lead down to the beaches. They have given the various stretches of beaches their current names. *Diamond Beach* is rather superior, while *Lagada Beach*, *Sunny Beach* and *Magic Beach* are quite plain. Sun loungers and sun parasols are available to hire above the beach at the restaurants, otherwise there is plenty of space on the sand to spread your towel. Only ⭐ *Polémi Beach,* to the east of *Magic Beach*, sets itself apart from the others: "Polémi Beach is exotic," says the guy hiring parasols,

INSIDER TIP
Bathe like Adam and Eve

and indeed nudist bathing is tolerated at this beach. *Access paths from the main road, each 0.6–1.3km long |* 🗺 *C–D 5–6*

WEST COAST BEACHES

7–14km / 15–35 mins from Kéfalos by moped

What lengths will you go to find the perfect beach? If no distance is too far, then four exceptional beaches await you in the far west of Kos. From the Ágios Ioánnis Pródromos monastery, *Kavo Paradiso Beach* can only be reached by jeep, motorbike or on foot. Lots of fine sand, few people, just a handful of sun loungers and parasols in summer and its spectacular rocky backdrop make this beach so special. There are no houses for miles around so you don't

INSIDER TIP
Truly remote

even need to wear your swimsuit if you don't want to.

The other three beaches are easily accessible by car. *Theológos Beach* is well signposted from the main road and features a very narrow strip of sandy and pebbly beach at the bottom of a steep cliff and a good restaurant. Before you reach Theológos Beach, the same road branches off to *Káta Beach* which is devoid of dwellings. Apart from the occasional professional surfer, you'll be left in peace here.

From Theológos Beach, follow the narrow track along the coast until you reach an extremely photogenic chapel at an otherwise inhospitable bay.

If you then follow the signs on the waste bins for 900m, you come to one of the island's most picturesque beaches, *Tripití Diamond Beach*. Fifty palm-covered parasols await you at this tiny sandy beach nestled between the rocks. Alongside the improvised miniature petting zoo (set up by the guy renting sun loungers), with chickens, geese, rabbits, sheep and donkeys, there are cold beverages for sale and an emergency toilet. Steps lead down to the beach which offers unspoilt views of the wide-open sea in front of you. *A–B 7–8*

INSIDER TIP
Beach at world's end

WHERE TO STAY IN THE WEST

RELAX ABOVE THE BEACH

The Diamandis family put their heart and soul into offering the best of Greek hospitality. At the *Panorama Studios (17 apartments | tel. 22 42 07 19 24 | panorama-kefalos.gr | €€)* a gourmet breakfast awaits every morning, with eggs laid by their chickens, cheese from their goats and home-made jams. On request, guests of this apartment house, set high above the Ágios Stéfanos Beach, have a hire car at their disposal, available on arrival at the airport. Enjoy a glass of wine every evening on your own balcony with views overlooking the bay and plain to Kéfalos and over the sea to Nissíros or even Kálimnos. The house lies 15 minutes away from Ágios Stéfanos

Beach and three minutes on foot to the bus stop. The proprietors speak English.

A POOL WITH A VIEW

The *Hermes Hotel (70 rooms | on the main road from Kámbos to Kéfalos | tel. 22 42 07 11 02 | hermeshotel kos.com | €€)* is situated halfway between the mountain village of Kéfalos and the Kámbos plain, so that it will take you 10 to 15 minutes on foot either uphill to the village or downhill to the beach. If you don't want to go out, you can stay on the pool terrace and enjoy the magnificent views across the bay. In the evening, there is often dancing, and the majority of guests are polite British holidaymakers.

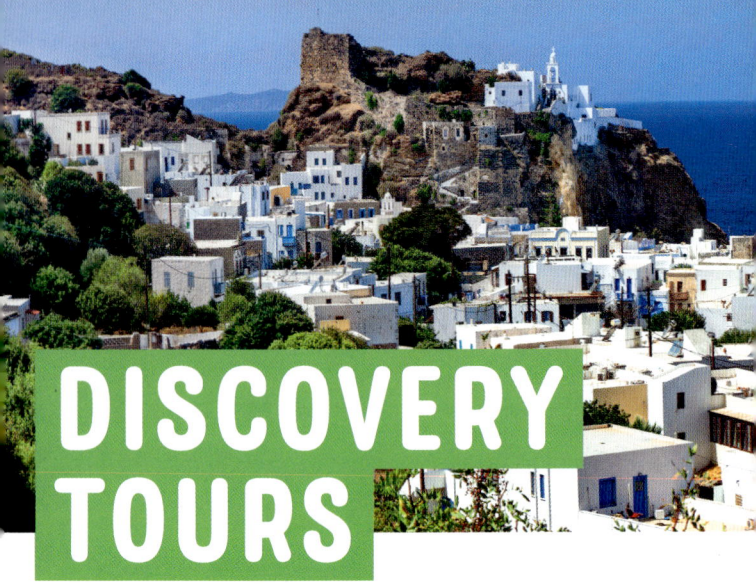

DISCOVERY TOURS

Do you want to get under the skin of the island? Then these discovery tours provide the perfect guide. They include advice on which sights to visit, tips on where to stop for that perfect holiday snap, a choice of the best places to eat and drink and suggestions for fun activities.

❶ KOS AT A GLANCE

- ➤ Ancient splendour in the early morning
- ➤ Bathing fun – swimsuit optional
- ➤ Thermal baths in the moonlight

📍	Kos Town	🏁	Kos Town
🔄	130km	🚗	1 day (2½ hrs total driving time)
ℹ️	Hire a car from 45 euros per day. Bring a head torch for night-time bathing in the thermal baths.		

The small island of Nissiros in picture-postcard blue and white

COFFEE AND KOAN HISTORY

Set off early from ❶ Kos Town ➤ p. 38 and *drive to the* ❷ Asklípion ➤ p. 60. In the balmy early morning air around 8.30am, the view of the coast of Asia Minor across the water is still clear. Enjoy your first cappuccino or espresso on the village square in ❸ Platáni ➤ p. 58, before you *head off on the main island road* to ❹ Antimáchia ➤ p. 81, the village at the heart of the island. At the Traditional House ➤ p. 81 in the village centre, you can travel back in time and discover the island's history.

GO WEST: A RUINED CHURCH, MONASTERY AND BATHING STOP

Afterwards, follow the call of the wild west. *It's a full 17km until you reach the next settlement*, Kéfalos, which stretches along the coastal plain. Right at the beach, you will find the beautiful ruins of ❺ Ágios Stéfanos Basilica ➤ p. 90, one of the many early Christian basilicas on the island. Stop briefly in the authentic village of ❻ Kéfalos ➤ p. 90 before you head into the isolated countryside around the abandoned monastery of ❼ Ágios Ioánnis Pródromos ➤ p. 94. Along the way, you will pass goats and sheep

❶ **Kos Town**		
	4km	7 mins
❷ **Asklípion**		
	1km	4 mins
❸ **Platáni**		
	20km	25 mins
❹ **Antimáchia**		
	15km	14 mins
❺ **Ágios Stéfanos Basilica**		
	4km	4 mins
❻ **Kéfalos**		
	6km	6 mins
❼ **Ágios Ioánnis Pródromos**		

15km · 14 mins

8 Magic Beach

grazing on the side of the road, and sometimes the farmers wave from atop their donkeys. From the monastery, you can enjoy the fantastic view that stretches as far as Mykonos on some days. Pass through Kéfalos *and take the main island road back*. A little detour to the peaceful **8 Magic Beach ➤ p. 96** offers the chance to cool off in the water. Don't worry if you don't have a swimsuit – nude bathing is permitted on the eastern section of the beach.

THE ISLAND CENTRE – A VILLAGE AND A CASTLE

It is an easy drive to the next destination, the large village of ⑨ Pýli ➤ p. 78 in the island's interior. You should visit the Tomb of Harmylos ➤ p. 79, not only because it is interesting from an archaeological point of view, but it is also in an idyllic position. The 400-year-old village fountain is a good place for a late mid-day break in the shade of the island's biggest fig tree. *Then continue to* ⑩ Old Pýli ➤ p. 80. To do so, *leave Pýli and follow the signs to Amanioú and Ziá. In Amanioú, continue straight on and do not turn left to Ziá. Park your car at the end of the paved road.* Then, it's time for a bit of exercise because the footpath through the forest up to the castle *takes about ten minutes to climb.*

INSIDER TIP
A huge fig tree

ADMIRE FRESCOES AND BROWSE ARTWORKS

Afterwards, *go back towards Amanioú,* but *make a sharp right towards Ziá.* This road takes you to ⑪ Lagoúdi ➤ p. 78. A narrow, cobbled street leads to the village church with its lovely frescoes. After enjoying the culinary delights served by Christina at I Oréa Elláda, you can take a look around the gallery attached to the café that sells local antiques, select jewellery at affordable prices and art works by the Flemish owner herself.

ENJOY THE BREATHTAKING SUNSET

The nearby mountain village of ⑫ Ziá ➤ p. 75 is so famous for its sunset views that numerous coaches stop here in the late afternoon every day. If you want to avoid the crowds, *hike uphill through the village past an old watermill* to the Sunset Balcony ➤ p. 77 restaurant.

THERMAL POOL AT NIGHT

If you are up for another adventure, then a very special treat awaits: a swim in the simple natural pool at ⑬ Embrós Thérme ➤ p. 57, where warm water from a healing thermal spring joins with the salty Aegean sea. It might be handy to have a torch to help find the way. Relaxed, but surely tired after your swim, it is time to head back to ① Kos Town.

20km	20 mins
⑨ Pýli	
6km	3 mins
⑩ Old Pýli	
5km	4 mins
⑪ Lagoúdi	
1km	1 min
⑫ Ziá	
24km	23 mins
⑬ Embrós Thérme	
11km	11 mins
① Kos Town	

❷ A BIKE TOUR OF THE FLAT NORTH

➤ Bathe along the way
➤ Watch wild flamingos
➤ Go riding

📍 Kos Town		🏁 Kos Town	
🔄 58km		🚲 8 hrs (4 hrs total cycling time)	
📶 Easy		↗ 200m	
ℹ️ Rental fee for a good bicycle approx. 10 euros			

CYCLE TO THE NORTH CAPE

Either rent a bike for the day near your hotel or in ❶ Kos Town ➤ p.38 at Moto Harley ➤ p.32. *Cycle down to Mandráki Harbour ➤ p.43 and turn left at the western end of the harbour road onto the wide cycle path on Odós G. Averóf. When it comes to an end, turn right and follow the road that runs along the beach to the north.* You will pass an old industrial area whose numerous beach cafés are popular meeting places for local young people. You can only dance here in the

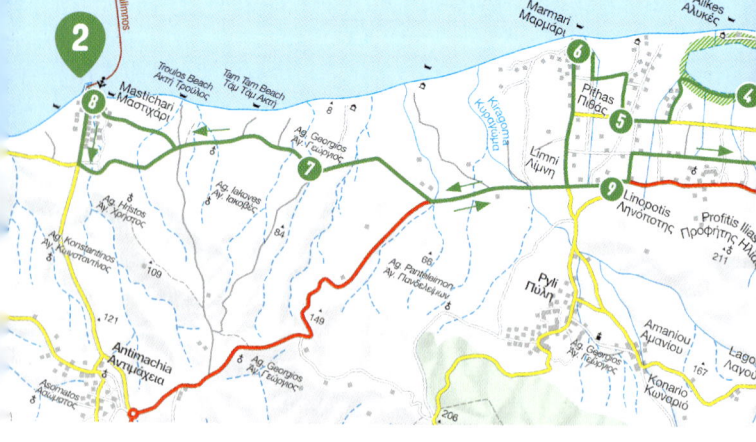

summer, though. When you can't go any further along this road, *turn left and follow the broad main road* through the district of **Lambí** to the sea. The northernmost tip of the island is marked by the flat ❷ **Cape of Ammoudiá**, which is now home to a military base and a beacon. The long sandy beach begins near the point and stretches to Mastichári. For the most part, the route continues near the beach, which means that you can stop for a swim every now and then.

TO THE SALT LAKE AND RIDING STABLES

The first town you will come to is ❸ **Tigáki ➤ p. 68**. At the *roundabout on the beach, go right down the road near the coast that leads past fast-food stalls and tavernas to Taverne Alikes. You will now cycle along the south side of the* ❹ **Alikés salt lake ➤ p. 68**. Much of the nature here is still very pristine. Well into early spring, you can watch as flamingos and other waterfowl catch fish in the salty lake. Be careful along the shoreline because the dry-looking soil often turns into a trap as the crusty surface hides patches of moist clay that will literally stop you in your tracks! At the *south-western corner of the salt lake, turn left on the broader track that will take you back to tarmac. Cycle along until you reach the southern edge of Marmári.*

INSIDER TIP
Mind the trap!

5km	13 mins

❷ **Cape of Ammoudiá**

10km	40 mins

❸ **Tigáki**

2km	6 mins

❹ **Alikés**

2km	9 mins

Don't miss out on a short, but refreshing break on the terrace of the café at **5** Erika's Horse Farm ➤ p.70, which also has a small petting zoo. If you want, you can even trade saddles for an hour or so and explore the area on horseback.

PAST THE CHAPEL AND INTO THE TAVERNA

Continue on to the resort town of **6** Marmári ➤ p.69. *Turn left onto the road that takes you to the main island road. Follow the main island road for 2km to the right and then turn onto the well-marked lane to Mastichári. Stop after approx. 2km, before the bend on the edge of a small hollow.* In this idyllic setting, you will find the ancient chapel of **7** Ágios Geórgios Loízos under an impressive umbrella of pine trees. The chapel is thought to be about 800 years old, but it was built with the remains of an early Christian basilica from the fifth/sixth century. In **8** Mastichári ➤ p.71 you can eat a good yet inexpensive lunch at the taverna Kalí Kardiá and then go just a few steps further to jump in the water off the sandy beach.

A TINY POND AND VENERABLE RUINS

The route back to Kos Town sometimes follows the way you came. *From the harbour of Mastichári, follow the main road to the south and just before the edge of town, turn left. After about 1.5km, you will meet the road you already know that leads past the church of Ágios Geórgios Loízos to the main island road. Follow the main road for about 3km,* until you see the tiny pond of **9** Linopótis on the right, which is home to a fair number of ducks and turtles who like to sunbathe around the edge.

After you go past the pond, turn left and then turn right again shortly thereafter. To the left, you can see the Alikés salt lake again, *and you will soon come across the cul-de-sac to Tigáki. Turn right here and follow the main island road towards Kos Town.* You will pass through the large, modern village of **10** Zipári with its simple cafés. On the other side of the bridge, *a path leads about 100m* to the ruins of the early Christian basilica of **11** Ágios Pávlos.

PAST THE CHAPEL – AND INTO THE SEA!

Continue along the main island road. After about 800m, a road forks off to the north towards the ⑫ Chapel of Ágios Ioánnis/St John, which is closed. You can't go inside, but it is still interesting to see that it was built on top of an early Christian crypt. *Go further along this lane to get back to the road near the coast,* which you already know from the beginning of the tour. *After 9km, you will get back to* ❶ Kos Town, but you might want to take another dip in the sea along the way.

0.5km	2 mins
⑫ Chapel of Ágios Ioánnis/St John	
12km	48 mins
❶ Kos Town	

❸ PICTURE-PERFECT VILLAGES & THE VOLCANO OF NÍSSIROS

➤ Sunbathe on the boat
➤ Take a walk on the "moon"
➤ Look for pumice

📍 Mandráki/Níssiros   🏁 Mandráki/Níssiros

🔄 40km   🚗 8-9 hrs (ferry 90 mins each way; approx. 40 mins total driving time)

ℹ️ Return boat ticket approx. 25 euros, hire car approx. 35 euros, moped approx. 12 euros (plus petrol). Boat tickets available at Mandráki Harbour, departure around 9am. You can also depart for Níssiros from Kardámena and Kámbos. Cars and scooters can be hired from *Nisyros Rent a Car & Motorbike Manos K. (tel. 22 42 03 10 29 | nisyros-rentacar.gr)*

ACROSS THE SEA TO THE VOLCANO

Níssiros has a population of about 1,000 people, divided among four villages. Tour boats and ferries dock at the main town of ❶ Mandráki. When you arrive around 10.30am, you can pick up your rental car directly at the harbour. It is located right on the *main island road. Bear left, follow the road along the sea, past*

❶ Mandráki	
13km	14 mins

the small thermal bath of Loutrá and *then turn right just before the tiny settlement of Palí. The lane winds up the cliff of the volcano.* Your first destination is the village of ❷ Nikiá on the edge of the crater. Some of the residents look out of their windows directly into the crater, while others look out to the sea. The only other place in Greece with such a constellation is the much more famous island of Santorini. The small volcano museum *(Mon–Sat 10am–8pm, Sun 11am–6pm | admission 4 euros, incl. caldera 8 euros)* is located next to the car park. A flower-lined *lane leads about 250m into the village*. The incredibly photogenic platía is the perfect place to sit in the small café tucked away between white houses.

GRAZING COWS AND SULPHURIC VAPOURS

Return to the road and head back for a bit until you come to the signs for the turn-off to the left down into the crater. This ❸ caldera is approx. 3km long and 1km wide, and the wall up to the edge is up to 698m high. One half of the crater is so green that cows graze on it, but the other half looks like a lunar landscape. Sulphuric vapours rise from several places, and you can often see bright yellow sulphur deposits. The approx. 350m-long and 250m-wide Stéfanos crater carved itself into the rugged side. There are four other secondary craters located nearby, but they are largely inaccessible. *The road ends in the middle of the crater* at a café. From here, you only have to walk a few metres to step into the Stéfanos crater, the most spectacular of the secondary craters.

RETURN FROM THE CALDERA TO THE SEA

Afterwards, *drive back up to the edge of the crater* and visit the second crater village of the island, ❹ Emporiós. Once you have enjoyed another view down into the crater, *head back to the coast*, and fill your tank just before the harbour at the only petrol station on the island before you return your hire car.

Now it is time to explore ❶ Mandráki on foot. It stretches for several hundred metres along the sea to the ruins of a castle belonging to the Knights of St John

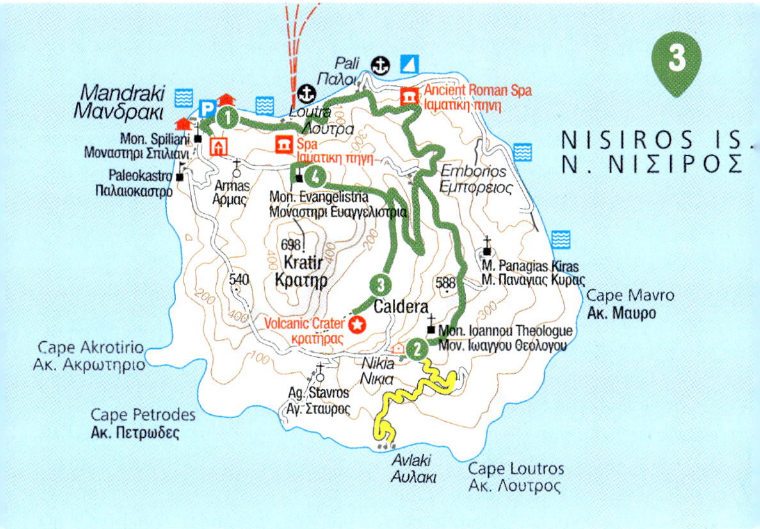

NISIROS IS.
Ν. ΝΙΣΙΡΟΣ

that sits atop a rocky point. On the way to the castle, you will pass by the tiny **beach of Mandráki** with its small 👯 playground. With a bit of luck, you can often find a pumice stone that has washed ashore from the mining island of **Gialí** across the way. On the grounds of the **castle**, you will find a church dedicated to the Virgin Mary, which is a popular pilgrimage destination in the first half of August. Around 2pm at the latest, you can eat a late lunch in one of the tavernas located along the shore. Or, if you prefer, you can head to the long village square and choose one of the cafés or restaurants whose tables and chairs are spread out under the tall trees. Please make sure to keep track of the time so that you won't miss your ferry (most leave around 4pm)!

11km   8 mins

❹ A MOUNTAIN-BIKE TOUR THROUGH THE HEIGHTS OF KOS

➤ Fitness required on steep ascents
➤ Take a break in an abandoned village
➤ Refuel at the island's best pastry shop

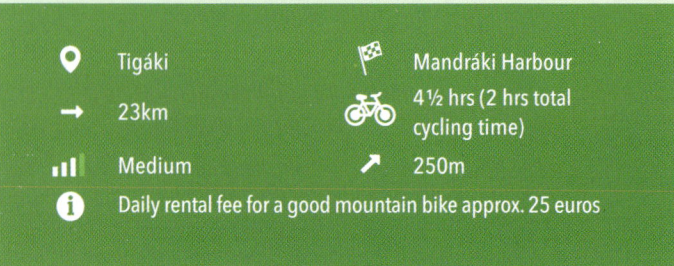

📍	Tigáki	🏁	Mandráki Harbour
→	23km	🚴	4½ hrs (2 hrs total cycling time)
📊	Medium	↗	250m
ℹ️	Daily rental fee for a good mountain bike approx. 25 euros		

❶ **Tigáki**

6km 24 mins

❷ **Lagoúdi**

1km 6 mins

❸ **Evangelístria**

1km 11 mins

❹ **Zía**

4km 22 mins

❺ **Ágios Dimítrios**

A BEAUTIFUL VILLAGE AND GREAT VIEWS

From ❶ Tigáki ➤ p. 68, *take the main island road to the right. It crosses over a dry stream bed and comes to another after about 500m. Just after the bridge, a small, tarmacked road branches off towards the interior of the island* up to ❷ Lagoúdi ➤ p. 78. As you pass through the lovely village, don't forget to stop and take a look at the village church. *Continue cycling uphill* to ❸ Evangelístria and take a well-deserved break on the village square. Afterwards, *the road winds up steeply to* ❹ Zía ➤ p. 75, which is a popular tourist destination. Bike up to the old town centre above the street of souvenir shops to the church (signs to Square Karídias) and treat yourself to another break around noon to enjoy the views from the terrace of the Sunset Balcony ➤ p. 77 restaurant.

ABANDONED HOUSES IN THE FOREST

Return to the souvenir street and go right. Pass by the animal enclosures of the Natural Park Zía ➤ p. 77 and leave all the hustle and bustle behind you. At first the tarmacked road is narrow, but then it widens, taking you *2.5km through a shady forest to the abandoned village* of ❺ Ágios Dimítrios. You can wander around the empty houses, visit the small museum and take a break in the traditional village *kafenío* Haihoútes, surrounded by the peaceful forest. From here, *the route is almost entirely downhill. Pass by the entrance to the municipal landfill;* you'll know when you're there thanks to the shreds of plastic blowing in the wind. *The route continues past the access road to the* Asklípion ➤ p. 60, for which you should plan a separate trip. Shortly thereafter, *you will come to the* ❻ village square of Platáni ➤ p. 58, which is home to an excellent pastry shop and several good tavernas.

FINAL PUSH TO THE HARBOUR

Head to the right from the village square and go past the local mosque. Continue about 700m further, then turn left at the next larger crossroads. Pedal on through Ampávris, a suburb of Kos Town, and you will come to the ruins of an aqueduct in ❼ Kos Town ➤ p. 38 near the Casa Romana ➤ p. 47. It is not far from here to ❽ Mandráki Harbour ➤ p. 43 where you can enjoy a mocktail to sustain yourself for the return journey to Tigáki.

7.5km	29 mins
❻ Platáni	
2.5km	10 mins
❼ Kos Town	
0.5km	2 mins
❽ Mandráki Harbour	

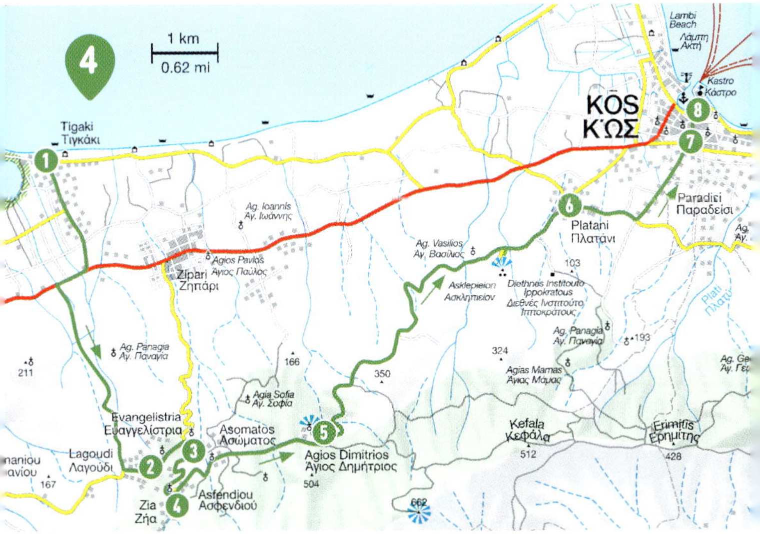

GOOD TO KNOW

HOLIDAY BASICS

ARRIVAL

GETTING THERE

Direct flights, including various budget carriers, connect Kos between May and October with numerous airports in Europe and the UK. In winter, you can only get there via Athens with *Olympic/Aegean (aegeanair.com)* or *Sky Express (skyexpress.gr).* Taxis wait at the airport (fare to Kos town approx. 40 euros), and there are bus transfers to Kardámena, Kéfalos, Mastichári and Kos Town *(3.20 euros | 50 mins | ktel-kos.gr).* In summer there are daily ferries between Kos and Piraeus and in the winter ferries run three times a week *(journey time 8–12.5 hrs | gtp.gr).*

TIME ZONE

Greece is two hours ahead of Greenwich Mean Time, seven hours ahead of US Eastern Time and seven hours behind Australian Eastern Time.

CLIMATE & WHEN TO GO

The season on Kos lasts from May to October. Outside that time, many hotels and most restaurants outside the capital are closed. In May, the water might be a bit cool for swimming, but nature is at its best, with beautiful blossom everywhere. In July and August, the mercury rises well above 30°C, hardly ever dropping below 20°C; strong winds can cool the air. Autumn offers the advantage of pleasantly warm swimming temperatures, but the disadvantage of largely dry and burnt vegetation. There is hardly any

+ 2/3 hours time difference

Kos is 2 hours ahead of GMT in winter, and 3 hours during summer.

Getting around on Kos is easy by car, bus, bicycle, mini-train or moped

rain between June and September, but some thundershowers.

GETTING AROUND

FERRIES & BOAT TRIPS
Car ferries and superfast ferries connect Kos Town with most islands of the Dodecanese, as well as with Turkish Bodrum. In addition, a car ferry and a fast ferry serve the Mastichári–Kálimnos and Kardámena–Níssiros routes. There are organised boat trips to Níssiros, Kálimnos and Bodrum.

HIRE VEHICLES
A large selection of bicycles, mopeds, scooters, motorbikes and cars may be rented in any holiday resort. To rent a car or a motorbike over 125cc you will need the national driver's licence for the relevant category and will have to be at least 21 years of age. Even taking out fully comprehensive insurance doesn't insure you against damage to the tyres or the undercarriage of the vehicle. Do call the police after even the tiniest accident, as the insurance won't pay otherwise. Unless indicated otherwise by signage, the maximum speed in built-up areas is 40kmh and on country roads it's 70kmh. At roundabouts, the rule "right before left" applies, unless indicated otherwise. Seatbelts have to be worn in the front seats. The blood alcohol limit for drivers is 50mg of alcohol per 100ml of blood; for motorbikers and caravanners it's 10mg! Parking offences start at 60 euros.

PUBLIC TRANSPORT
Scheduled buses are the most useful and best value public transport option.

Even the longest distance (Kos Town–Kéfalos) costs no more than approx. 5 euros. The long-distance bus terminal in Kos Town is at *Odós Kleopatras 7*. For up-to-date time schedules and prices visit *ktel-kos.gr*.

Local buses serve the island's capital, as well as connecting it with the hotel resorts of Lambí and Psalídi. They also run to the Asklípion via Platáni and to the Embrós Thérme via Ágios Fókas. The central terminal for local buses is at Aktí Miaoúli.

If you intend to explore Kos Town and its surroundings, you may benefit from the *All-Day Ticket (10 euros)* from Elma-Ko. As well as touring the entire town, it allows you to use the buses and mini-trains *(trenáki)*, which run between Tigáki, Ágios Fókas, Kos Town and the Asklípion.

Tickets are on sale on the buses and trains. (Please make sure that you carry enough small change.)

RESPONSIBLE TRAVEL

It doesn't take a lot to be environmentally friendly while travelling. Don't just think about your carbon footprint while flying to and from your holiday destination *(myclimate.org, routerank.com)*, but also about how you can protect nature and culture abroad. As a tourist, it is especially important to respect nature, look out for local products, cycle instead of drive, save water and much more. To find out more about eco-tourism, visit: *ecotourism.org*

TAXIS

All taxis on Kos are metered. You can either stop one on the road, find one at taxi stands or call one out by phone, for an extra charge of about 3 euros. Prices are fixed by the state and are relatively low; a taxi from the airport into Kos Town costs about 40 euros.

EMERGENCIES

EMBASSIES

There are no consulates on Kos; any queries need to be addressed to the embassies of your country in Athens.

BRITISH EMBASSY

Odós Ploutarchou 1 | 10675 Athens | tel. 21 07 27 26 00 | ukingreece.fco.gov.uk

US EMBASSY

Vasilisis Sophias Avenue 91 | 10160 Athens | tel. 21 07 21 29 51 | athens.usembassy.gov

EMERGENCY SERVICES

Dial *112* for the police, ambulance and fire brigade.

HEALTH

All larger settlements on the island have a pharmacy. UK citizens can theoretically be treated for free by doctors if you present the Global Health Insurance Card *(gov.uk/global-health-insurance-card)*. However, in practice doctors do so reluctantly and it is better to take out private travel insurance that covers medical issues, including repatriation.

FESTIVALS & EVENTS
ALL YEAR ROUND

JANUARY
Epiphany (all coastal towns): the priest throws a cross into the sea for the daring to retrieve, followed by celebrations

MARCH
Carnival Monday (Pláka): picnics and barbecues in the forest

APRIL/MAY
Ágios Geórgios (Pýli): church feast day with horse racing in the main street
Good Friday (all villages): ceremonial processions around 9pm.
Easter Saturday (all villages): Easter Mass at 11pm is a fixture for most Koans

JUNE
Ágios Nikítas (Níssiros): church feast day in the harbour town of Mandráki

AUGUST
Ippokratía (Kos Town): culture festival with events at the Odéon and Casa Romana

Honey Festival (Antimáchia): on a Sunday around the historic museum windmill
Wine Festival (Evangelístria): on the last Sunday of the month on the church square
Dormition of the Virgin Mary (Kéfalos): feast day with music and dance on the evening of 14 August
Ágios Ioánnis Pródromos (Kéfalos): major church feast when many visitors spend the night from 28–29 August celebrating on the large square of this remote monastery

SEPTEMBER
Stavrós (Pýli): morning church service in the tiny chapel above the tomb of Harmylos on 14 September

OCTOBER
Climbing Festival (Kálimnos): three-day festival for rock climbers on the neighbouring island *(climbingfestival. kalymnos-island.gr)*

ESSENTIALS

ADMISSION FEES

State-run museums and archaeological sites are free for children and young people (up to the age of 25) from EU countries and those with international student card; senior citizens enjoy a discount. Between November and March, admission is free for all on the first Sunday of the month.

CUSTOMS

UK citizens can bring out goods worth up to £390, but there are limits on alcohol and tobacco products. See *gov. uk* for updates. EU citizens may import and export duty-free goods for personal use, incl. 800 cigarettes, 10l of spirits and 90l of wine. Residents of the US do not have to pay duty on articles purchased overseas up to the value of $800, but there are limits on the amount of alcoholic beverages and tobacco products (see *cbp.gov*).

INTERNET & WIFI

Many hotels and cafés offer free WiFi hotspots for guests. Slow internet connections are relatively rare. When data roaming, absolutely make sure that you are not logged into a Turkish network because they tend to charge high usage fees!

MONEY & CREDIT CARDS

The local currency is the euro. There are numerous ATMs (cash points). Credit cards (Visa, MasterCard) are accepted most places. Bank opening hours are Monday–Thursday 8am–2pm and Fri day 8am–1.30pm.

PUBLIC HOLIDAYS

1 Jan	New Year
6 Jan	Epiphany
March	Carnival Monday
25 March	National Holiday
April/May	Greek Good Friday
5 April/May	Greek Easter
1 May	Labour Day
June	Whitsun
15 Aug	Assumption of the Virgin Mary
28 Oct	National Holiday
25/26 Dec	Christmas

SHOP OPENING HOURS

Most local shops open Monday–Saturday 8.30am–2pm and Tuesday, Thursday/Friday 6–9pm; supermarkets open Monday–Saturday approx. 8am–9pm. In summer, souvenir shops open daily approx. 9.30am–11pm.

TELEPHONE & MOBILES

You can buy OTE phone cards at kiosks, but phone booths on Kos are not properly maintained and often don't work.

UK mobile operators are no longer obliged to provide free data roaming in EU countries; check your contract before you leave home. NB: Around the east of Kos, mobiles sometimes connect to expensive Turkish network providers. Greek mobile numbers start with a 6. International country codes: UK +44, Ireland +353, US/Canada +1, Greece +30.

TIPPING

Greeks simply leave their tips on the restaurant table when they depart. Please note that amounts of less than 50 cents are seen as an insult.

TOILETS

In order to avoid clogging up potentially old drainage systems, please don't throw your toilet paper into the loo, but into the bucket or waste-paper basket provided. This rule even applies to luxury hotels.

TOURIST INFORMATION

There is no official tourist information on Kos. Events are advertised with posters.

GREEK NATIONAL TOURISM ORGANISATION (UK/ IRELAND)

4 Great Portland Street | W1W 8QJ, London | tel. 020 7495 9300 | visit-greece.gr

GREEK NATIONAL TOURISM ORGANISATION (USA/CANADA)

800 Third Avenue, 23rd floor | New York, NY 10022 | tel. 212 421 5777 | visitgreece.gr

WEATHER ON KOS

High season
Low season

	JAN	FEB	MARCH	APRIL	MAY	JUNE	JULY	AUG	SEPT	OCT	NOV	DEC
Daytime temperature	15°	16°	17°	21°	25°	30°	32°	33°	29°	25°	21°	17°
Night-time temperature	7°	8°	9°	11°	15°	19°	21°	22°	19°	15°	12°	9°
Hours of sunshine per day	5	5	7	9	10	12	13	12	11	8	6	4
Rainy days per month	14	10	8	3	3	0	0	0	1	6	7	13
Water temperature in °C	17	16	16	17	19	21	23	25	24	22	20	18

☀ Hours of sunshine per day   ☂ Rainy days per month   ≈ Water temperature in °C

WORDS & PHRASES
IN GREEK

SMALL TALK

Yes/no/maybe	ne/'ochi/'issos	Ναι/ Όχι/Ίσως
Please/Thank you	paraka'lo/efcharis'to	Παρακαλώ/ Ευχαριστώ
Good morning/good evening/goodnight!	kalli'mera/kalli'spera/ kalli'nichta!	Καλημέραμ/ Καλησπέρα!/ Καληνύχτα!
Hello/ goodbye (formal)/ goodbye (informal)!	'ya (su/sass)/ a'dio/ ya (su/sass)!	Γεία (σου/σας)!/ αντίο!/Γεία (σου/ σας)!
My name is …	me 'lene …	Με λένεÖ …
What's your name?	poss sass 'lene?	Πως σας λένε?
Excuse me/sorry	me sig'chorite/ sig'nomi	Με συγχωρείτε / Συγνώημ
Pardon?	o'riste?	Ορίστε?
I (don't) like this	Af'to (dhen) mu a'ressi	Αυτό (δεν) ουμ αρέσει

SYMBOLS

EATING & DRINKING

Could you please book a table for tonight for four?	Klis'te mass parakal'lo 'enna tra'pezi ya a'popse ya 'tessera 'atoma	Κλείστε ασμ παρακαλώ ένα τραπέζι γιά απόψε γιά τέσσερα άτομ
The menu, please	tonn ka'taloggo parakal'lo	Τον κατάλογο παρακαλώ
Could I please have … ?	tha 'ithella na 'echo …?	Θα ήθελα να έχω …?
more/less	pjo/li'gotäre	ρπιό/λιγότερο
with/without ice/ sparkling	me/cho'ris 'pa–go/ anthrakik'ko	εμ/χωρίς πάγο/ ανθρακικό
(un)safe drinking water	(mi) 'possimo nä'ro	(μη) Πόσιμο νερό
vegetarian/allergy	chorto'fagos/allerg'ia	Χορτοφάγος/ Αλλεργία
May I have the bill, please?	'thel'lo na pli'rosso parakal'lo	Θέλω να πληρώσω παρακαλώ

MISCELLANEOUS

Where is …?	pu tha vro …?	Που θα βρω …?
What time is it?	Ti 'ora 'ine?	Τι ώρα είναι?
How much does... cost ?	Posso 'kani …?	Πόσο κάνει …?
Where can I find internet access?	pu bor'ro na vro 'prosvassi sto índernett?	Που πορώμ να βρω πρόσβαση στο ίντερνετ?
pharmacy/ chemist	farma'kio/ ka'tastima	Φαρακείοιμ/ Κατάστημ καλλυντικών
fever/pain /diarrhoea/ nausea	piret'tos/'ponnos/ dhi'arria/ana'gula	Πυρετός/Πόνος/ Διάρροια/Αναγούλα
Help!/Watch out! Be Careful	Wo'ithia!/Prosso'chi!/ Prosso'chi!	Βοήθεια!/Προσοχή!/ Προσοχή!
Forbidden/banned	apa'goräfsi/ apago'räwäte	Απαγόρευση/ απαγορέυεται
0/1/2/3/4/5/6/7/8/9/ 10/100/1000	mi'dhen / 'enna / 'dhio / 'tria / 'tessera / 'pende /'eksi / ef'ta / och'to / e'nea / dhekka / eka'to / 'chilia / 'dhekka chil'iades	ηδένμ/ένα/δύο/τρία/ τέσσερα/πέντε/έξι/ εφτά/οχτώ/ εννέα/ δέκα/εκατό/χίλια/ δέκα χιλιάδες

HOLIDAY VIBES
FOR RELAXATION & CHILLING

FOR BOOKWORMS & FILM BUFFS

📖 BLUE SKIES & BLACK OLIVES

In a moment of mad impulse, journalist, broadcaster and TV presenter John Humphrys bought a semi-derelict cottage overlooking a glorious bay in the Aegean. With his cellist son, Christopher, he set about renovating the property and recording the "survivor's tale of housebuilding and peacock chasing in Greece". (2009)

📖 ODYSSEUS & PENELOPE: AN ORDINARY MARRIAGE

An entertaining novel by the classicist Inge Merkel (translated by Renate Latimer) that retells the myth from an unusual perspective.

🎥 SIGNS OF LIFE

German film director Werner Herzog produced his first feature film on Kos at a time when there were only a handful of tourists on the island. The story is set during the Second World War and includes many beautiful shots of Kos Town and the island scenery. (1968)

🎥 ZORBA THE GREEK

Although this iconic film (starring Anthony Quinn) was shot in Piraeus and predominantly on Crete, it was instrumental in forming our view of the Greek way of life in general. The *sirtaki* can still be seen at countless folklore events. (1964)

PLAYLIST

0:58

II ROTTING CHRIST –
THE APOCRYPHAL SPELLS
The latest release (2023) by the titans of Greek rock.

▶ **GIÓRGOS DALÁRAS –**
I MEGALÍTERES EPITÍHES TOU
A selection of the best songs by the "Greek Bruce Springsteen".

▶ **MARÍA FARANDOÚRI –**
MARGARÍTA MAGARÓ
Talented singer María Farandoúri interprets one of the best songs by famous composer Míkis Theodorákis.

▶ **FRANKOSYRIANÍ**
The biggest hit of Rembétiko underground music can be heard in many clubs.

▶ **ÉLENA PAPARÍZOU –**
MY NUMBER ONE
Greece's one and only winning song from the 2005 Eurovision Song Contest.

The holiday soundtrack is available at **Spotify** *under* **MARCO POLO** *Greece*

Or scan the code with the Spotify app

ONLINE

J GREEKA.COM/DODECANESE/KOS/
Greek travel community with videos, articles, photos and blogs

USTKOS.CO.UK
This is the liveliest community for the island. Here you can read the experiences of predominantly British holidaymakers on Kos as well as find reviews and tips regarding numerous hire car firms, hotels, bars and restaurants.

VISITGREECE.GR/ISLANDS/DODECANESE/
A website with information on the island's history, culture, cuisine and beaches.

VISITKOSGREECE
The island's official Instagram account doesn't offer much in terms of solid information but it has many beautiful photographs.

TRAVEL PURSUIT

THE MARCO POLO HOLIDAY QUIZ

Do you know what makes Kos tick? Here you can test your knowledge of the little secrets and idiosyncrasies of the island and its people. You will find the correct answers below, with further details on pages 18 to 23 of this guide.

❶ Greek saints are like government ministers: each one has his or her own department; which department is Saint Markélla responsible for?
a) Finance
b) Hip pain
c) Travel

❷ Which group of islands does Kos belong to?
a) Dodecanese
b) Cyclades
c) Balearics

❸ Apart from drinking coffee, what is the favourite coffee-table pastime for many Greek men?
a) They play *távli*
b) They play *tabla*
c) They do crosswords

❹ Which famous physician was born on Kos?
a) Aristotle
b) Christian Barnard
c) Hippocrates

Answers: 1b, 2a, 3a, 4c, 5a, 6c, 7b, 8b, 9a, 10c

A prominent Koan who healed with the help of the gods

❺ What do Greeks mean by the word *paréa*?
a) A group of friends
b) A beach towel that is wrapped round the hips
c) Old people who have become homeless as a result of many pension cuts

❻ What must a Greek-Orthodox priest never ever do?
a) Marry
b) Have children
c) Shave his beard

❼ What role did "tongues" play for the order of the Knights of Saint John?
a) They were the commander's traditional favourite dish
b) They were administrative divisions according to language within the order.
c) They were the emblem on the knights' shields

❽ Which Koan citizen was cited as an exemplary European by the Luxembourg prime minister?
a) An island mayor who wanted to make Kos the European capital instead of Brussels
b) An island baker who distributed bread to refugees free of charge
c) A pub landlord who offered British holidaymakers free beer

❾ With which hand does an Orthodox Christian make the sign of the cross?
a) The right hand
b) The left hand
c) Both hands

❿ A form of EU already existed 700 years ago. What was its capital?
a) Brussels
b) Rome
c) Rhodes

INDEX

WE WANT TO HEAR FROM YOU!

Did you have a great holiday? Is there something on your mind? Whatever it is, let us know! Whether you want to praise the guide, alert us to errors or give us a personal tip – MARCO POLO would be pleased to hear from you. Please contact us by email:

We do everything we can to provide the very latest information for your trip. Nevertheless, despite all of our authors' thorough research, errors can creep in. MARCO POLO does not accept any liability for this.

sales@heartwoodpublishing.co.uk

PICTURE CREDITS
Cover photo: AWL Images: Ken Sciclun
Photos: K. Bötig (123); R. Hackenberg (49); huber-images: D. Erbetta (6/7, 24/25), R. Schmid (86/87); F. Ihlow (46, 70/71); Laif: T. Gerber (12/13, 32/33, 58, 80, 84, 96); Laif/IML(79); E. Laue (64/65); Lookphotos: Avalon.red2 (43); F.-M. Frei (91), Jorda (35), I. Pompe (56, 93); mauritius images: J. Clasen (10, 55), M. Habel (2/3, 38/39, 53, 73, 118/119), S. Plant (9), Waldkirch (30/31), J. Warburton-Lee/K. Scicluna (23); mauritius images/age fotostock: J. Wlodarczyk (back cover flap); mauritius images/Alamy: G. Balfour Evans (75), A. Bandurenko (34), M. Czekajewski (76), P. Forsberg (31), Freeartist (98/99), A. Mastoris (19), R. Ramos (27); mauritius images/United Archives: De Agostini/G. Dagli Orti (120/121), Rudolph (14/15); picture-alliance (20); picture-alliance/Eibner-Pressefoto: Drofitsch (50); picture-alliance/Westend61: S. Rothe (94/95); S. Randebrock (26/27); Shutterstock: Nejdet Duzen (44, 60/61), Christos Ignatiadis (113), Tom Jastram (11), Anna Jedynak (110/111), Cem Ozer (front cover flap1), George Papapostolou (62, 69), Manolis Smalios (8)

3rd Edition – fully revised and updated 2024
Worldwide Distribution: Heartwood Publishing Ltd, Bath, United Kingdom
www.heartwoodpublishing.co.uk

Authors: Klaus Bötig
Editor: Corinna Walkenhorst
Picture editor: Anja Schlattere
Cartography: © MAIRDUMONT, Ostfildern (pp. 36–37, 100, 102–103, 109, back cover, pull-out map); © MAIRDUMONT, Ostfildern, using data from OpenStreetMap, licence CC-BY-SA 2.0 (pp. 40–41, 57, 66–67, 83, 88–89)
Cover design and pull-out map cover design: bilekjaeger_Kreativagentur with Zukunftswerkstatt, Stuttgart
Page design: Langenstein Communication GmbH, Ludwigsburg

Heartwood Publishing credits:
Translated from the German by Thomas Moser, Susan Jones; Jennifer Walcoff Neuheiser, Kathleen Becker
Editors: Rosamund Sales, Kate Michell, Felicity Laughton, Sophie Blacksell Jones
Prepress: Summerlane Books, Bath
Printed in India

MARCO POLO AUTHOR
KLAUS BÖTIG

Germany's most-trusted author on Greek travel topics is also an honorary citizen of the island of Kos – possibly just because he was available when the mayor was looking for a suitable candidate! As a result of this honour, Klaus feels obliged to find those parts of the island which make Kos a gem for adventurous and curious visitors who love the genuine Greece.

DOS & DON'TS

HOW TO AVOID SLIP-UPS & BLUNDERS

DON'T ORDER FISH UNSEEN
In Greece, fresh fish and shellfish are sold at exorbitant prices, and often by weight. To avoid unpleasant surprises, ask for the kilo price and try to be present when it's being weighed too.

DO WATCH FOR LANGUAGE NUANCES
When at a restaurant, please don't ask for a "serviette" because this word means a sanitary pad in Greek. What you really want is a *chartopetsétta*. And remember that "no" is *óchi* in Greek, while *nee* means "yes".

DON'T FALL FOR A CHEAP BODRUM TRIP
At Mandráki Harbour you can pick up a ticket for a trip across to Turkey for as little as 25 euros, including a guided tour of Bodrum. The problem here: the tour goes mainly to carpet dealers and shopping centres, where the promoter pockets high commissions.

DON'T SUCCUMB TO A KIR ROYAL
Jewellery dealers like to offer their customers a glass of whisky, ouzo, champagne or kir royale. If you accept, it might be wise to postpone your purchase for a second visit…